HOLY TOAST

7 REASONS MINISTERS LEAVE MINISTRY

What Church Leaders and Members have said:

"This is an easy read that is very thought-provoking. In the weeks that have passed since reading Mike's book, I find myself spending more time in prayer for my preacher and trying to find ways to be a better friend and be more supportive of him and his family."

"This book made me want to hug a minister. It's an insightful work with an important message for all church people. There were plenty of laugh-out-loud bits as well as stop-and-think bits. Overall, it was highly readable. It will be a very useful book to many."

"It was good to get a minister's perspective on some of these issues. I think most churches would recognize themselves in these stories and believe that this book will have broad appeal to leaders and congregations who are interested in forging more trusting, effective, serving relationships with each other."

A very insightful read. I appreciate Mike's honesty and direct approach. Over the short history of paid ministry, church "society" has created a set of work expectations that do not fit, nor are they fair, in the present culture and time. This book caused me to rethink what are acceptable expectations and how to support a very challenging work! I pray this will help make not only our ministers and their families healthier, but our congregations healthier also.

Dedicated to all my ministry colleagues both current and former. Thanks for all your years of service in the Kingdom.

CONTENTS

THIS IS NOT A PREFACE

I have been in and around ministry my whole life. I grew up as a minister's son in a Christ-loving and God-honoring house. I went to church *a lot*. I attended a Christian high school. I counselled at camps and interned with different churches every summer. After graduation I entered a one year internship before completing my degree in Biblical studies. I have experienced much of the good and some of the not-so-good that comes from working with and for a church. In many ways my life has always revolved around ministry. Therefore, I, more than many of my future ministry colleagues, knew exactly what I was getting into. That being said, I had no idea what I was getting into.

Throughout my internships and professional career I have spent time ministering in churches of handfuls and hundreds. I have been in the really rural and the ultra-urban. I have filled the role of youth minister, associate minister, lead minister and the 'jack of all trades whatever needs to be done you're the only guy around to do it' minister. There have been days when I loved my job and days when I hated it. Times when I couldn't imagine doing anything else and times when I would have done just about anything else. These experiences, along with my relationships with so many wonderful people who have invested so much of their lives in the work of the Kingdom, inspired me to write this book.

One day as my wife and I were discussing our disappointment in seeing yet another dear friend walk away from ministry I began ruminating on why I believed this was becoming such a seemingly common occurrence. Perhaps she was just tired of listening to me pontificate, but Michelle said, "You should write a book about it." After 18 years of marriage I know when it is pointless to argue (out loud) so in the following weeks I sketched out the basic points that would become the *7 Reasons Ministers Leave Ministry*.

SIDENOTE: Just to be clear, my disappointment was not in the least with my friend who had just decided to leave ministry. My frustration and heartbreak were solely with whatever situations, structures or systems made him, and too many others I knew, feel like leaving ministry was their only viable option for the sake of their family and their sanity.

The church-minister relationship can be complex waters at times. I pray this book can be a useful resource as you navigate your way through. At the very least, I hope it will serve as an avenue to open up dialogue between churches and ministers leading to more effective working relationships beneficial to everyone involved.

The previous paragraphs explain why I wrote this book, but why are you reading it? Don't get me wrong, I'm glad you are. Not because I have illusions of grandeur or aspirations of a Pulitzer. I am thankful you have begun to read this book for a couple reasons – none of which have to do with my current spot on the New York Times best seller list. So before we go any further, let me be clear about a couple things.

First of all, the fact that you have picked up a copy and read even this far indicates to me that you are someone who cares about the health and effectiveness of the church and I am very grateful for it. The more churches are filled with people who are invested in making things better instead of just looking for what they can get out of it the better off the mission of the Kingdom will be. So thanks for being one of those people.

Second, odds are if you are reading this book you belong to one of two camps. The first group is composed of church leaders (with and without title) and regular members who care deeply about their minister. The second group is made up of ministers and ex-ministers. Depending on which of these two groups you are in, you will likely read this book very differently. So please allow me to speak a few words to each of you specifically before we get started ...

Dear Church Member,

Thanks again for reading. I know I've said it several times already, but it's worth repeating. The fact that you're willing to take the time and initiative to pick up and read a book like this speaks volumes about your heart. Clearly you are someone who cares about the physical, spiritual, emotional and mental well-being of your minister. I've had people like you in my life and I cannot begin to tell you how much I value and appreciate them. I imagine your minister feels the same way about you.

Let me begin by saying, this book is not meant to be a criticism of you or a two hundred page rant on how hard done by your minister is. That is not the intent at all. I also do not mean to suggest that your job, whatever that may be, is without its own frustrations, stresses and anxieties. I'm sure your job has plenty of all of those things.

However the reality is, for whatever reason (that's a great discussion for a whole other book), the church now finds itself in a place where full time paid ministers are stressed out, burnt out and dropping out. I believe there are systems and structures built into the way we 'do church' and the expectations we put upon our ministers that are at worst the cause and at best amplifiers of the issues that have produced this modern reality. Your minister may be working to reshape some of these things in your church (both out of a desire to see the Kingdom grow and simple self-

Dear Ministers,

Hi guys. I'm glad you picked up this book. It says to me you haven't given up. You haven't become so frustrated and fed up that instead of reading this book you started throwing it at people in your church (even though the thought may have crossed your mind). Odds are, if you ARE reading this book, you are likely dealing with some frustrations and stresses in your ministry. If you're not, you must still be in your first week on the job.

Some of you picked this book up hoping that it would have all the answers for your current irritations and anxieties. Some of you bought this book hoping it would finally open the eyes of your leaders to how difficult your job really is. Some of you are reading in hopes that what lies between these covers will help you make your final decision whether to stay or go. Some of you have already moved on from ministry and are reading these pages just to hear the voice of someone who understands what you went through.

I don't know if it will be able to do all those things for all of you, but what I most hope this book will be able to do is to help you identify what issues are most challenging for you and give you a medium to enter discussions with your church leaders about how to work together to improve things.

Ministry is not, and will never be an easy calling. It can be difficult, demanding and sometimes unfair. The reality is, for numerous reasons, the church finds itself in a place where the role and expectations of a modern, full time, paid minister can be extremely challenging. And while it is great for our congregations to be more aware of what preservation) or he may not even know where to begin. Either way, he needs your help to pull it off.

Before NASA sends astronauts into space they run them through a battery of tests and training exercises to prepare them for their journey. The scientists and techs at NASA do their best to replicate everything from the four Gs of force experienced at lift off to the weightlessness of space. I have no idea what either of those things feel like. However, the more I read descriptions of astronauts' experiences and learn about the measures that have been taken to try and help spacemen and spacewomen function effectively on their missions, the more I understand and empathize with them. The better I grasp the challenges they face. When Astronaut Chris Hadfield describes liftoff as being "shaken in the jaws of a gigantic dog...like a gorilla was squishing you and then threw you off a cliff," (Reddit - Dec 13, 2013) I get an idea of what it is like even though I've never actually taken off in a rocket ship myself (yet). His book strives to give you a sense of what it's like to do something you've never done before. Not to complain about the G-forces or the fact that normal toilets don't work in zero gravity, but to merely share this and several other things you may have never realized before unless you've actually been to outer space. I hope you find the experience as useful as - but far more pleasant than - a ride on the Vomit Comet (a real thing, I kid you not).

One last thing: Stop. Pray. Then read on!

ministry is like, it is really the underlying structures and systems of church life that need to be revisited and revised. That will not be a short or easy journey. The reality is the bulk of the weight of that mission will fall on your shoulders and there are some vital things that need to happen in your heart and life if you are going to be able to stand up under all of that, (but that's a discussion for another book).

I recall a discussion with a mentor of mine several years ago. We were discussing whatever my current frustration with my church was (I don't actually recall the specific issue). He asked me if I thought there was any way that this particular aspect of my congregation could ever change.

I replied with an uber-confident, "Maybe, someday, I guess." Then he asked if I was willing to do what would need to be done to make that happen.

Ugha. I don't recall what I actually told him, but my real answer was "No, I really don't think I want to." I hope you will read through this book, consider the issues discussed and open up dialogue with your church leaders about how to make both you and your church as healthy and effective as it can possibly be. Hopefully you will come up with an honest and genuine response much better than mine was that day.

One last thing: Stop. Pray. Then read on!

18

A WHOLE NEW WORLD

Okay, I know you really want to jump ahead to the **7 Reasons** (if you didn't jump ahead to Reason #1 right off the start), but please stick with me for a moment. I don't know how to explain this other than simply blurting it out, so here goes: You don't know what it's like to be in ministry unless you've been in ministry. You just don't.

I've had the opportunity to go to India several times to do mission work. One of the highlights of the trip for me is observing first-timers when they initially encounter a culture so vastly different than home. In preparation for the trip we always advise people about what to expect. We tell them stories and show them pictures. We do everything we can think of to describe what they will encounter. We tell them about the sanitary conditions, rudimentary accommodations, diverse bathroom arrangements and the extreme poverty. Regardless of what we do in advance, by the time we land in Kolkata, go through security and immigration, get our luggage, make our way out of the airport, drive a couple miles and arrive at our hotel all the newbies are in a state of shock.

Even though we did our best to describe the blaring sounds and pungent smells. Even though we tried to explain the masses of people and the absence of personal space. Even though we attempted to prep them for the experience of driving on Indian roads, best described by one first time visitor as MarioKart on acid. All the pictures, videos, stories and warnings we could give in advance were no substitute for walking off the plane and being hit by the heat, the humidity and the humanity! Even those who have been on mission trips to other places and therefore anticipate an easier adjustment are often blown over by the sights, sounds and smells they experience. Before arriving they simply could not fathom a place with that many people and that much poverty where they eat that much rice.

There are certain things in life that you simply cannot fully understand unless you've actually experienced them first hand. I think serving in full time ministry is one of those things. Ministry is unlike any other occupation. We can draw some parallels to other careers here and there, but they are limited. It doesn't mean my job is better or holier than yours, it's just really unique. For that reason, I need you to trust me on a few things. I've got no horse in this race. I don't get paid commission on any raise your preacher gets after you read this book. So, please believe me when I describe situations from a minister's perspective I have no angle to work. I'm giving an honest representation of ministry as I have experienced it myself and heard others describe it. You may think "It's really not like that," or "It shouldn't be like that," or "It doesn't need to be that way." Perhaps it doesn't, but it often is. "Surely it's not like that in our church!" Yeah, it probably is.

A life in ministry brings all sorts of challenges and issues that have quite possibly never even crossed the mind of those not in ministry. Let me give you a very simple example of what I mean. We were a single vehicle family for a long time. We were determined to put off getting a second car as long as we possibly could simply because the cost of purchasing, maintaining, insuring and fueling another vehicle is rather hefty. However this created some challenges for us particularly on Sunday morning. When I began working at my current church I had a wife, a two and a half year old and a one month old. As all of you know, especially those of you with small children, sometimes getting to church on time can be a bit of a struggle. I know you know this because I see you at every church I go to (including my own) as you limp in 10 or 15 minutes after the start of service with a diaper bag on your shoulder, holding on to one rug-rat in front of you by the collar, dragging another ankle-biter behind you like a sack of potatoes and looking like you just went three rounds with a grizzly bear. I feel your pain, believe me. However, in my case things were a little more complicated.

As minister I have things to take care of on Sunday morning which means I have to be at the building 30 minutes or more before the rest of you start to show up. I am blessed at our church that I'm not responsible for unlocking all the doors, turning on all the lights, setting out communion and shoveling the overnight snow. Many ministers are assigned these tasks as well which makes their start time even earlier. I still have to arrive early enough to get all my tasks done, get mic'd up for the sermon and put out any last minute fires that erupt, all in time to stand in the foyer and mingle with members and visitors as they come in. The challenge comes when not everyone in our house is ready to leave at the time I need to leave at. When this happens at your house, you just bear down and get people ready to go as soon as you can and then slip into the back pew as discretely as possible. That's not really an option for me. This is not only my job (which we all must be punctual for) but it is also the primary worship time for our church. If I'm not there to do the things I need to do the whole morning could be off kilter. Not to mention if I'm scrambling and running around like a chicken with his head cut off before service (or during the first few minutes of it), it is incredibly hard for me to be focused and in the right head space when sermon time comes around, let alone engage in the worship time in any meaningful way. Therefore the pragmatic thing to do is make sure I'm at the building early, even if it means leaving the house before the rest of my family is ready.

However, the flip side of the coin is that I'm also a father and husband who is responsible for the spiritual wellbeing of my wife and kids. As such, I feel compelled to stay home and help herd the cats until we're all ready to go. It is important to me that no one in my house miss out on the joy and encouragement from gathering with the church on Sunday for worship. It is important to me for my kids to be in Sunday School and learn the foundations of our faith and the basics of the Bible. It is important to me that my kids don't grow up feeling like church is what you do only when it is convenient or you don't sleep in too late. Not to mention, people notice when my family isn't there. People ask where they are and why they didn't come. And if it happens often enough some may even start to question and criticize. Therefore, as a one car family, many weeks I was faced with this Sunday morning dilemma: Do my job well and leave my wife and kids at home or be a good dad and get my family to church.

I share this example not to whine about having to show up early for church nor to highlight my family's need for more discipline in our time management. The reason I've included this story in this book and in this chapter in particular is because it is a great illustration of the principle being discussed. Odds are the dilemma described above is one you have never had to face. In fact, I suspect the thought of having to make that choice has never even crossed your mind. Why should it? That's not your reality – but it is mine. My experience isn't more valuable or saintly than yours, it's just different. That's what this book aspires to do: share perspective. My number one goal is to help you look into the world of your minister and hopefully walk away with a deeper insight into his reality. For the record, I did finally find a solution to this conundrum: we bought a second car.

<table>
<tr><td>

FOR MINISTERS ONLY:

Never underestimate the value of living within easy walking, biking, bussing, go-carting or pogo-sticking distance of your church building. You will save hours every month in lost commuting time, it gives you a built in opportunity for exercise (which is invaluable when you have an often sedentary job) and it can relieve the stress of this type of situation.

</td></tr>
</table>

Ministry simply doesn't fit into any other mold. So avoid paralleling things to where you work or a job someone you know has or even your own experience as a church member or volunteer leader. At some levels those parallels hold true, but at many others they simply don't. This book hopes to show you how things look and feel from the minister's side of the fence. If you really have a hard time believing me, go ask your minister.

WHAT THE STATISTICS SAY

There are plenty of statistics out there about ministers and their jobs. Some may be more accurate than others. I've included a few below from reputable sources. Certainly not all of these stats will apply to the minister at your church, but the numbers say they apply to most. And although your minister may be in the small percentage to which a certain stat does not apply, it would be foolish to believe he is in that same small percentage on _all_ the stats. (If he is, you should ask him to pick out your lottery numbers, because he clearly knows how to defy extreme odds). It may seem like a lot of numbers to wade through and there is some repetition but I wanted to give you multiple sources for credibility sake and to show that these issues are not isolated anomalies.

According to the New York Times (Aug. 1, 2010)

"Members of the clergy now suffer from obesity, hypertension and depression at rates higher than most Americans. In the last decade, their use of antidepressants has risen, while their life expectancy has fallen. Many would change jobs if they could."

- **13%** of active pastors are divorced.
- **23%** have been fired or pressured to resign at least once in their careers.

- **25%** don't know where to turn when they have a family or personal conflict or issue.
- **25%** of pastors' wives see their husband's work schedule as a source of conflict.
- **33%** felt burned out within their first five years of ministry.
- **33%** say being in ministry is an outright hazard to their family.
- **40%** of pastors and **47%** of spouses are suffering from burnout, frantic schedules, and/or unrealistic expectations.
- **45%** of pastors' wives say the greatest danger to them and their family is physical, emotional, mental, and spiritual burnout.
- **45%** of pastors say they have experienced depression or burnout to the extent they needed to take a leave of absence from ministry.
- **50%** feel unable to meet the needs of the job.
- **52%** of pastors say they and their spouses believe being in pastoral ministry is hazardous to their family's well-being and health.
- **56%** of pastors' wives say they have no close friends.
- **57%** would leave the pastorate if they had somewhere else to go or some other vocational skills.
- **70%** don't have any close friends.
- **75%** report severe stress causing anguish, worry, bewilderment, anger, depression, fear, and alienation.

- **80%** of pastors say they have insufficient time with their spouse.
- **80%** believe pastoral ministry affects their families negatively.
- **90%** feel unqualified or poorly prepared for ministry.
- **90%** work more than 50 hours a week.
- **94%** feel under pressure to have a perfect family.
- **1,500** pastors leave their ministries each month due to burnout, conflict, or moral failure.
- Doctors, lawyers and clergy have the most problems with drug abuse, alcoholism and suicide.

According to FASICLD (Francis A. Schaeffer Institute of Church Leadership Development).

- **100%** of pastors we surveyed had a close associate or seminary buddy who had left the ministry because of burnout, conflict in their church, or a moral failure.
- **90%** of pastors stated they are frequently fatigued, and worn out on a weekly and even daily basis.
- **89%** of the pastors we surveyed also considered leaving the ministry at one time.
- **57%** said they would leave if they had a better place to go – including secular work.
- **77%** of the pastors we surveyed felt they did not have a good marriage!

- **75%** of the pastors we surveyed felt they were unqualified and/or poorly trained by their seminaries to lead and manage the church or to counsel others. This left them disheartened in their ability to pastor.
- **72%** of the pastors we surveyed stated they only studied the Bible when they were preparing for sermons or lessons. This left only **38%** who read the Bible for devotions and personal study.
- **71%** of pastors stated they were burned out, and battle depression beyond fatigue on a weekly and even a daily basis.
- **38%** of pastors said they were divorced or currently in a divorce process.
- **30%** said they had either been in an ongoing affair or a one-time sexual encounter with a parishioner.
- **26%** of pastors said they regularly had personal devotions and felt they were adequately fed spirituality.
- **23%** of the pastors we surveyed said they felt happy and content on a regular basis with who they are in Christ, in their church, and in their home!

According to George Barna, Focus on the Family, and Fuller Seminary:

- **1500** pastors leave the ministry each month due to moral failure, spiritual burnout, or contention in their churches.

- **50%** of pastors' marriages will end in divorce.
- **80%** of pastors feel unqualified and discouraged in their role as pastor.
- **50%** of pastors are so discouraged they would leave the ministry if they could, but have no other way of making a living.
- **80%** of seminary and Bible school graduates who enter the ministry will leave the ministry within the first five years.
- **70%** of pastors constantly fight depression.
- Almost **40%** polled said they have had an extra-marital affair since beginning their ministry.
- **70%** said the only time they spend studying the Word is when they are preparing their sermons.
- **60%** to **80%** of those who enter the ministry will not still be in it 10 years later
- **10%** of those who enter ministry in their 20s will stay in ministry until retirement
- **70%** of pastors do not have close personal friends, and no one in whom to confide.
- **78%** said they were forced to resign from a church at least once. **63%** they had been fired from their pastoral position at least twice.
  - **52%** stated the number one reason was organizational and control issues. A conflict arose forcing them out based on who was going to lead and manage the church-pastor, elder, key lay person, faction, ...

- **24%** stated the number one reason was their church was already in such a significant degree of conflict, the pastor's approach could not resolve it (over 80% of pastors stated this as number two if not already stated as number one, and for the rest, it was number three!).
- **14%** stated the number one reason to be the church was resistant to their leadership, vision, teaching, or to change, or their leadership was too strong or too fast.

Despite the overall impression of "only working 30 minutes a week" and "throwing together his sermon on Saturday night"* ministers are statistically stressed, exhausted and discouraged. His occupation is demanding and hard on his family and will ultimately burn him out until he leaves the ministry and sometimes the church altogether.

SIDENOTE: By the way, your minister will likely smile and chuckle when you say stuff like that (*), maybe even say it himself at times, but inside it probably stings.

This would not be an attractive job description for any profession, *but in the church of all places, it simply should not be so.* The church should be setting the standard for what an employer should be.

Whether it is with secretaries, custodians or ministers the church should be the one showing the rest of the world "This is how you care for your employees. This is how you put the person ahead of the bottom line." And although some of the stresses and challenges of ministry may simply be inherent to the job, the church should be committed to doing whatever it can to minimize and counteract those elements. I believe many times our failure to do so as a church comes not from a lack of desire or intent but from a simple lack of understanding. The very fact you are reading this book proves you have the desire. My task in these next pages is to offer some ministerial perspective and expand your understanding. Good luck to the both of us in that quest!

WHAT DO YOU KNOW ABOUT IT?

I know what you're thinking: *"Who does this guy think he is to tell me anything? He doesn't know me. He doesn't know my church. He doesn't know our leaders. He doesn't know our minister. So what does he think he knows?"* Fair enough. I don't know you or your church or your leaders or even your minister. That's why I wrote a book for *YOU* to read and decide for yourself instead of walking into your church on Sunday morning and declaring your minister is about to quit. I'm not his union rep, I want you to be. Your minister needs someone to be his advocate and I want you to be the person in your congregation who steps up and speaks up at the next opportunity and says "Hey everyone, I know you love our preacher as much as I do, and if we want to keep him around, there are some issues we need to seriously take a closer look at." Based on the fact you bought this book in the first place – unless your minister bought it for you - I'm wagering you want to be that person too. (Technically you may not *WANT* to be that person, but you do want to make sure *SOMEONE* is and therefore you will either do it yourself if need be or buy another copy of this book and put it in the hands of someone you think can be that person in your church).

SIDENOTE 1: I say "buy another copy" rather than "lend out your copy" not as a thinly veiled ploy to up my book sales, but because I think it would be valuable for whoever you share this book with to read fresh pages and come to their own conclusions, not being led by your highlighting and margin notes (which I highly encourage you to scribble in). That way they can make up their own mind about all these things.

SIDENOTE 2: If someone else has bought you a copy of this book and given it you, you now know exactly what they are hoping will happen when you read it, right? They want you to be that someone. (If they've highlighted this block for you, then you know they're really serious.)

In my experience, most ministers are far more likely to quietly walk away than make demands. In fact, your minister more than likely feels like he _can't_ do it himself. Ministers are supposed to be humble and selfless. To insist on, or even merely request, something more or different would be unministerly. Besides, we expect our ministers to be spiritual leaders in our congregation. We don't expect them to say "I need some time away because my spiritual well is completely dry right now." Part of their ability to do their job is based on the congregation having confidence their minister has a sound and stable faith. Not to mention that if a minister were to insist on getting a raise, every time he preached a sermon on tithing or sacrificial giving he would feel the burn of each and every skeptical eye in the audience. His ears would ring with the unspoken – at least for now – thoughts of those in the pew. "Oh yeah, like you did when you demanded the big pay hike last spring?" Some of those concerns may be factual, others merely perceived, but either way these are very real to your minister and will most likely keep him from effectively being his own advocate.

FOR MINISTERS ONLY:

I know I just said you aren't going to be your own advocate or you may even feel like you can't be your own advocate, but you need to be your own advocate. Tell your leaders how you really feel and how the work you do affects you and your family. Talk to them about where you are at and what they can do to help preserve your spiritual health and your ministry. Ask them to read this book or at least let them know which of the **7 Reasons** are weighing on you. I know it's not comfortable or easy. I have not done it as often or as well as I should have in my own ministry career. However, if you don't do it, it is very possible no one else will and I'd hate to see that happen to you.

It's not like other ministers can advocate for your minister either, because we all know a rising tide lifts all boats, right? So when I lobby for better benefits on a fellow minister's contract everyone knows in the back of their minds next time my contract is up for renewal the expectation will be for me to get at least the same perks as the other guy got. Ex-ministers, on the other hand, have nothing to gain by advocating for current ministers and therefore their input should be seen as unbiased, however it is just as easily interpreted as sour grapes over whatever it is they blame for "driving them out of ministry."

Who does that leave? You. Joe or Jane congregation member. John or Jill board member. Jack or Janice elder or elder's spouse. It falls to you to do what needs to be done to ensure your minister has a long, healthy, productive and kingdom-blessing career working with your congregation to the glory of God. Amen.

That being said, if you are going to read any further and take the following pages with any kind of weight whatsoever, you likely want to know if I know what I'm talking about. Well, here's my resume for authoring this book - you can decide for yourself if you are interested in hearing what I have to say.

- My father started in ministry the year I was born and is still on staff at a church. That's 40+ years of being a preacher's kid with a front row pew, literally at times, for observing and experiencing ministerial life.
- I have spent the past 19 years in full time church ministry
- Have I ever thought about quitting? Many times.

- Have I ever come close to actually quitting? Very.
- How close? Hold this page up vertically and look at its thickness – yeah, about that close.

For the record, the examples I share in the following chapters are not bitter complaints, merely stories I hope will help illustrate for you what your minister's life is like. Most of the antagonists, for lack of a better word, in these illustrations are good-hearted, God-loving people whom I appreciate very much. And that's part of what makes all of this so complicated. You work at a secular job surrounded by people with all sorts of moral and religious convictions, so you are not shocked or surprised when people are careless or thoughtless or mean or manipulative or only out for themselves.

But your minister works in what should be a utopian environment surrounded by kind-hearted, God-fearing, Christ-following believers. There shouldn't be any problems or struggles or misunderstandings there, right? Perhaps when the first android church is established that might be true, but as long as the church is full of people I'm afraid these challenges will still exist and need to be addressed. Not because members are maliciously out to destroy their ministers, but simply because, as you may have heard, you can't fully understand ministry unless you've actually been in ministry. When we don't understand, we misunderstand which is when problems start.

However, the primary impetus for writing this book, is not my own frustrations. This is not my passive-aggressive way of attacking my elders or my church or leveraging them to give me a big raise. Do not assume this is merely a report card on my particular congregation. There are many of these areas in which I believe our church excels and that makes me very proud to be a part of this group.

No, I have a very different motivation for penning this particular book.

My father is an extreme rarity. He has spent the past 41 years serving as a minister in the Lord's church. That, in and of itself, is laudable. But what really sets him apart is that all those years he has logged are not only within the same denomination, but with the same congregation where even now, after entering semi-retirement, he remains on staff offering a couple days each week. Even as I type that paragraph I feel like I should write Guinness (the record book, not the dark ale). That is a feat virtually unheard of and rarely matched – which I think says something really wonderful both about my dad and the congregation he serves.

You likely don't need me to tell you 40 plus years is not the norm. If you are a typical North American evangelical church, you likely cycle through a new minister every four to seven years on average. My denomination is a relatively small one, so we tend to be fairly well aware of what goes on in the other congregations in our fellowship in our part of the country at the very least. Therefore it is a common joke when a preacher retires or moves out of the region, it is time for the *Sermonizer Shuffle.* (Okay, maybe I'm the only one who *actually* calls it that, but I'm hoping the name will catch on). The effect is especially pronounced when the vacant spot is located in one of the bigger churches. You can easily chart the trickledown effect as preacher one moves from church B to church A. Then preacher two moves from church C to church B. And preacher three moves from, well, you get the idea. A chain reaction shuffles the ministerial deck of our denomination and everyone starts all over - until the next round. And some of that is normal, I guess. As ministers gain more experience they often move 'up' to larger congregations. Youth Ministers become Associate Ministers. Associate Ministers become Lead Ministers. It is the circle of pastoral life. Cue Simba.

There are many things we could say about or learn from that cycle, but the more disturbing pattern I have observed emerging with increasing frequency, among my peers especially, sees ministers not just moving from one ministry position to another but leaving ministry all together. They are abandoning the pulpit for UPS, retail jobs or the IT department. It is not a matter of needing to start fresh in a new church but rather making the choice (not in any way lightly) to leave ministry altogether and search for new employment with an employer who is, to put it bluntly, not the church.

I can name off the top of my head a shockingly long list of ministers in my peer group, in my part of the country, from my particular denomination who have boxed up their commentaries and handed in their PowerPoint clickers in the last decade. I know most of these guys personally and have talked with them at length. They come from churches of a wide range of sizes. From congregations at different positions on the liberal/conservative scale. They have held various roles and positions within their respective congregations. Some still worship with the churches they resigned from. Whatever compelled them to move on they were convinced it could not be addressed merely by moving to a new church. In other words, _their church_ wasn't the problem, it was _the church_ - particularly what the church requires of and gives to its ministers. It is common in any profession for some people to decide their current job isn't really a good fit for them and therefore they choose to pursue a different career path. This is normal and in many cases a good move for everyone concerned. But what we're talking about here is something different. We're talking about godly men and women, who at one point felt unmistakably called to full time ministry, choosing to walk away from their church office and seek employment elsewhere.

I don't claim to have all the answers to this issue,

and I'm pretty sure that if someone were to stumble upon the answers none of them would be easy fixes. What I hope to offer you on the remaining pages is a glimpse into the world of full time ministry from someone who has been there and done that. I will also do my best to give you some suggestions on how you can bless, care for and minister to your minister. I hope to be the voice of someone who understands, at least in general terms, what it is like to be the minister at your church. At the same time I'm someone who has absolutely nothing to gain by encouraging you to adopt new policies and approaches when it comes to the men and women who have devoted themselves to working for God's kingdom as church staff members.

So, with that heart and desire in mind, I offer you the *7 Reasons Ministers Leave Ministry*. Some ministers are closer to leaving than others. Your minister may feel some of these things strongly and others things not so much. But if you don't know if or how close your minister is to quitting and you don't know which of these seven factors are prompting him to ask himself if this is really what he should be doing, then I beg you, for Christ's sake, keep reading with an open mind and heart. Don't go in with your own agenda or intent on debunking ministry myths. Read on with the desire to understand and empathize. Read on with the goal of seeing the church and your minister differently. Discuss the issues with your leadership people. Ask your minister if he thinks any of this is true or it's all bologna made up by some nut-bar trying to sell some books. Ask your minister which of the **7 Reasons** he has wrestled with in the past. Which ones are weighing him down now?

My greatest hope is for churches to use what they discover on the following pages, along with much prayer and the discernment of the Spirit to care for and nurture their ministers in such a way that leads to a new and unimagined era of growth and effectiveness in the Kingdom. Looking at the world around us, I am convinced the church's mission is going to get more difficult before it gets any easier. If that is the case, we are going to need our best men and women serving in our congregations, able to be at their best and equipping us for the task the Lord has given us.

WHAT YOUR MINISTER SAID

Okay, I may not have actually talked with *your* minister, but I talked with a bunch of them. In fact I gave some of them copies of the manuscript for this book. The comments below are a sample of the responses that came from a cross-section of ministers. Some served with relatively large churches, others with smaller ones. Some from more progressive congregations, some from more traditional ones. Some are still in ministry, others have moved into other fields. They live across North America and come from both inside and outside my own denomination. They represent as diverse a group as my rolodex would allow me to poll. These people are not from the big megachurches, but from ordinary congregations just like yours, (unless of course you attend a megachurch – but I'm sure the principles apply just as much there as anywhere else). Here is a small sampling of what they had to say about what you are about to read:

All seven stressors will impact a preacher's life and family at some point of ministry. Sometimes all seven come to bear at the same time. If I had one section to work on first it would be "trust." This is developed over time and usually requires either intentionally invested time or successfully enduring a crisis together. When "trust" is mutually extended and high then many of these other issues can be addressed. A second key is for the preacher to be a life-long learner and for the congregation to bless those growth opportunities by investing finances and time into your minister. Thanks for helping to make many aware of the blessings and challenges of ministry.

– In ministry 30 plus years

As I read through this book, it made my stomach sick. Not because it is poorly written, but because the things that Mike describes brought back many similar experiences from my career: Hurtful comments... Careless criticism... Expectations that no one else in the congregation had to live up to (or would even put up with)... Pressure to "do more", "be more" and "produce results" in an environment where production was mostly out of my hands (After all, "Only God who makes things grow" – 1 Corinthians 3:7). Many times I considered moving to a different congregation or even to a different profession. It scares me to think about how many times I was on the edge of a complete emotional collapse. I was "burning out" at an unbelievable rate. My salvation came in the form of a former minister who was forced out of ministry by circumstances similar to mine. He helped the congregation understand what I needed. They responded and that allowed me to find the joy of this work again. I hope this book does for you what my former minister friend did for me and our congregation.

– In ministry for 25 years

Thanks for a great job in chronicling what is the greatest problem in the Christian church today. Something very important is very broken. And in my lifetime, I have seen nothing offering a true Christ-honoring solution. I am now seventy. I began my work as a paid "minister" when I was 17 continuing until I was 48. I worked 31 years as a paid staff member. Over the years I have encountered numerous men who, like myself, have been abused and almost derailed by the "Holy Toast Syndrome" which this book describes extremely well. Some got better. Some did not. I pray that this work will be an important spark to light a fire which says: "We have had enough. God is not pleased, we are losing ground. Let us seek God and do something new that really does the work of the ministry, and let us keep praying and trying new things until God shows us what to do.

*— **Left ministry after 31 years***

This book is for real. My hope and desire is for all ministers, elders, church leaders, and members of our fellowship to read this book. Mike addresses many of the problems that are encountered in ministry with humour, tact, and respect. This book is about working solutions and enhancing Christian relationships. I beg you to read it.

*— **In ministry for 12 years***

It is difficult to find young people today who desire to give their lives to full-time Ministry. Books like "Holy Toast" awaken us to some of the reasons why. Mike articulates well many of the challenges of local church ministry. I hope this message will enlighten church members to the realities of paid ministry and motivate them to come alongside their ministers to create fresh options for church leaders (paid and unpaid) to work together.

– In ministry for 20 plus years

I think this could really help open eyes if people were actually to read it and process it. I personally love seeing where my people do what you suggest and cringe over the parts where they don't - criticism, extreme expectation, 'undermeaning'. I pray God uses it to strengthen his Family for the next generation. My secretary has heard from her brother, who ministered, some of the struggles he's had. She is now a champion of minister's needs in our congregation. I hope this book has the same impact for Christians worldwide!

– In ministry for 18 years

Excellent book based on real life experiences that resonated with me. Mike hits the nail on the head with the 7 reasons. Churches don't have to lose ministers if they are willing to listen and make adjustments as the Spirit leads. I have left ministry but did so with grace and thankfulness and am still attending the congregation that journeyed with my family through 12 rewarding years together. The greatest suggestion in this book is finding and/or creating your own support network. For me, it made ministry not only possible, but at times very enjoyable."

– Left ministry after 20 years

I appreciate so much Mike having the courage to write this book. He has done an excellent job of explaining the unique intricacies of being a minister without resorting to whining or seeking sympathy. I believe his motivation is to make the Church healthier through mutual understanding by corresponding parts of the body. God has expressed openly how happy he is when his children get along. I think Mike has written a book that will help us get along and work together to further the kingdom of God. I pray that many people will read this book and do it in the spirit in which Mike wrote.

– In ministry for 29 years

Holy Toast is not about theories or speculations nor is it some kind of rant by a disgruntled preacher. It is instead an insightful reflection on years of ministry that honestly probes some of the hard questions about minister fatigue and burnout. From inside the skin of someone who's walked the walk the reader is taken to sacred places that are often shielded from public view. Many of the 'why' questions people are reluctant to ask are given legs and a heartbeat in this down to earth reality check. To read it objectively will surely provide a starting place for discussions that have been too long neglected by ministers, church leaders and congregations.

– In ministry for 40 plus years

REASON #1

Volunteers

Let me sum this one up in a nutshell: How many people at your church show up late on Sunday morning? Our congregation averages about 150 each Sunday. One Sunday morning about a month ago I took a photo with my cell phone that showed nine minutes left on our pre-service slideshow and every chair in the auditorium was vacant. On most weeks, at ten minutes prior to worship beginning we average less than a dozen in our auditorium. Less than 50 in our building. The other two-thirds of our group straggle in over the next half hour. I'm pretty sure we're not unique on this point. As the minister, I want everyone there on time so:

1) Our worship time is energetic and engaging not scattered and sparse,

2) Each member gets the full blessing of encouragement from the service (seriously, when you show up half an hour late all you get is to listen to me drone on and on – you miss all the really good stuff!)

3) Because for us, like many churches, Sunday morning is our main connection time with people from outside our church. It is many people's first impression of what our congregation is like and a dozen people in 200 chairs doesn't really send the right message.

As minister I am partially responsible for our worship, our fellowship, our outreach and our ability to retain visitors who attend our services. I even feel the weight of the parts of our worship service I am not officially responsible for. And what can I do to get people to show up on time? Put a note in the bulletin; announce it from the front; offer pre-service coffee and donuts; change the start time; make an impassioned plea at the start of my sermon - in other words, pretty much nothing. I've seen all these things done at churches with negligible effect. The reality of it is people will show up when they want to show up.

I recently told a friend, "Sometimes I feel like everything I do is like getting people to show up on time for church." Your minister is held responsible, directly or indirectly, for the success or failure of numerous programs and goals in your church. Whether or not your church is being effective or ineffective in various areas eventually, one way or another, usually falls on your minister. Which would be a heavy enough burden to bear, especially when you consider most ministers believe the well-being and health of their congregation is not just important at job review time, but it is a responsibility given to them by God Almighty who will hold them accountable for what they have or haven't done with what He has given them. However, the weight is magnified exponentially when you realize as minister you have very little control over what actually happens – yet are still responsible for the outcome.

Much of ministry feels very similar to this. It feels that way because your minister is stuck dealing with a group full of volunteers. Well meaning, good hearted, God-loving volunteers, sure, but still volunteers. Every project he begins, every event he plans, every sermon he preaches is dependent on volunteer leaders and volunteer participants.

- Your minister wants your church to be more service oriented so he plans a canned food drive. Is he successful? Depends who shows up. Depends who brings cans of food
- Your minister wants your church to be more effective at outreach so he schedules a special "Invite Your Neighbour" coffee house night. Is he successful? Depends on who shows up. Depends on who invites their neighbor.
- Your minister wants your church to know their Bibles better so he teaches a class before worship on Sunday. Is he successful? Depends on who shows up (and stays awake).
- Your minister wants to increase fellowship in your church so he schedules monthly potlucks. Is he successful? Depends on who shows up. Depends on who brings food and if there are still devilled eggs left when I go through the line – seriously, the devilled eggs are a deal breaker.

So much of what your minister is called to do and accomplish depends on whether or not his congregation of volunteers shows up and participates. So much of it depends on whether or not activities delegated to other leaders actually get done, on time and in a decent manner.

Having the patience to work with volunteers is a special skill set in its own right, but when your success or failure, your effectiveness or ineffectiveness, your competency or incompetency is dependent on whether or not volunteers show up or complete the tasks requested of them, well that's a whole new level of anxiety right there.

Imagine if you will, your co-worker has booked the next month off for vacation time. You know that some of the time she will be in town and some of the time she will be away. The first day of her vacation you get an email from your boss with a list of things he needs you to accomplish by the end of the month. Many of the things on your list require jobs to be done only your co-worker is trained to do. Even if you could do those tasks, the sheer volume of the work load is too much for you to complete on your own. What do you do? Well, you could call your co-worker up and tell her you need her help. You could ask her if she could come in and do a few things. You could insist that it's really important or promise to cover shifts for her when she returns from vacation, but that's about it. You don't have the authority to make her come in. You don't have the authorization to pay her double time and a half or even her regular salary. All you can do is ask nicely and hope she shows up. Hope she does enough of what needs to be done and does it well. At the end of the month your boss is going to evaluate how well the job was done and it will be your neck on the line if he's not satisfied. Now imagine your job is like that every week, every month, every year.

SIDENOTE: If you just read the paragraph above and thought to yourself, "That's ridiculous. No business would ever operate in this manner. How would you possibly get anything done?" then you read it right.

In a world where people are getting busier and busier, where people feel more tired and stretched, where life is filled with a plethora of activities, your minister is reliant on a shrinking group of volunteers who are becoming increasingly unavailable. If this were a business we would simply cut services or remove items from our production line. But the church still needs to accomplish the same things it has always needed to accomplish. Your minister can't stand up front on Sunday morning and announce, "Our volunteer hours are down so this fall we will be cutting our outreach department. Those who have been volunteering time for outreach will be reassigned to either service projects or building maintenance." I'm guessing this announcement probably wouldn't go over very well in your church. If it would then you've got a whole different set of problems to worry about.

Your minister has absolutely no leverage to use and his charm and charisma will only get him so far, for some of us that's not very far at all. He can use guilt or pound the pulpit, but the effects of those strategies are short lived and not exactly positive. The only weapon he has in his motivational arsenal is to try and build a relationship with you so you care enough to respond when he makes a request. That's a lot to ask. It doesn't happen quickly and it doesn't happen with 50, 150, 500 people at once. And the burden placed on him is only magnified by knowing he is being assessed by how well – if at all – others carry out his plans and designs.

If you have ever been tasked with recruiting people to teach or assist in your church's Sunday School program, you likely know a little bit of what I'm talking about here. Virtually every church I've been to, regardless of its size, has the same struggle. Leaders beg and plead and shoulder tap and beg some more for people to volunteer to teach kids classes. They often find themselves so desperate they end up using people whose hearts are in the right place but really don't have adequate skills or training to teach the class effectively. The quality and caliber of the education program is limited by the volunteers the leaders are able to recruit. Occasionally a fed up leader will announce because teachers can't be found the class for a certain age group will be cancelled until further notice. Perhaps someone will volunteer which gets them out of a jam, at least until next session. Perhaps the leaders receive criticism for cancelling the class or countless opinions (usually from people yet to volunteer) about how classes should be restructured or done differently. Often, the leaders themselves end up covering all the classes they could not find volunteers for.

Now imagine the above scenario represented the vast majority of activities you were charged with achieving. To complicate matters further all the volunteers for all your various activities must be drawn from the same pool of people. Which means whenever you succeed in recruiting a volunteer to one task you have just made finding a volunteer for the next task that much harder. Not to mention your credibility, your capability and your career are all on the line based on whether or not you can get enough people engaged in all the areas under your purview and equip, train and manage them well enough that they fulfill their role with a high degree of competency. Man, I'm exhausted just writing that out, let alone having to do it week after week after week.

WHAT MIGHT HELP?

This is one of those issues where the problem may in fact be systemic to how we do church compounded by the hectic schedules of modern life. Many people talk of "volunteer fatigue" – essentially where people are tired of volunteering for stuff. Although I may not dismiss the idea altogether, I am prone to think the problem is really more just plain, old, regular fatigue. It's not that people are volunteering too much and are therefore tired of doing so, it's more that people are *doing* too much and are therefore too tired to volunteer. There are some pretty significant culture shifts that need to take place in the way we live our lives before we'll see much change in this area.

At the same time, the church will always be a volunteer led and run organization. Whether it's showing up for worship services (on time or at all), joining small groups, teaching kids classes, participating in service projects, reaching out to neighbors or countless other activities the church is involved in, the bottom line is the effectiveness and success of these activities will continue to depend largely on volunteer leaders and entirely volunteer participants.

So, what might help alleviate this issue? Here are a couple of ideas to make life a lot easier and less stressful for your minister:

- **Make time.** Rearrange your life so your schedule is not always maxed out. Create some buffer zones so that when a need does come up you don't feel so overwhelmed by everything else that even the thought of volunteering to assist exhausts you. This isn't just for your minister, although he may benefit from it, but it's also a great thing for you and your family. You won't feel so burdened by the things you are already committed to and will less frequently feel guilty for the things you have to turn down. Your life will be more in balance and you will be happier for it. I'm not saying it will be an easy change to make or preserve, but it is worth it.

- **Volunteer readily.** Be quick to volunteer when you are able. People, especially in church, have this notoriously frustrating habit of sitting back and waiting to see who else volunteers first before offering their own services. Often people will say "Let me know if you can't find anyone else," or "If no one else will do it, then come back and ask me again." Although it is great you are willing to be the failsafe person it would be even greater if you were the *first to sign up and I brought a friend with me too* kind of person.

- **Take it into account.** Whenever you assess your minister's efforts, always evaluate the impact the volunteers (or quality of or lack thereof) had on the overall effectiveness. If you are disappointed at the meager turn out and mild success of a certain project, just imagine how the guy who put his time and effort into putting the whole thing together and doing everything in his power to make it succeed feels about it. Let your minister know you understand that despite his best efforts people just didn't show up or follow through and there's only so much he can do about it. This is not shock to him of course, it is something he already knows all too well. However you have no idea how affirming it will be to him to hear you know it too.

Just today I cancelled a spiritual retreat I had been planning for people in our church. I thought it would be an excellent idea. I was sure there were a lot of people who would really benefit from what we were planning to do. I promoted, I hyped, I encouraged and I cancelled. There simply weren't enough people signed up to participate. From talking with people I'm sure many saw the value of the retreat and could see how it would be a good thing to be a part of, but in the end only a tiny handful signed up to go. So what do I make of that? Just another day at the office.

REASON #2

Hijackers

Several years ago I was leading our small group program. I had logged many hours recruiting leaders, building groups and preparing curriculum. During the Christmas break, I was told one of the groups had found some different material they decided to use instead of the format I had laid out. At first I tried not to take it personally and as such I didn't resist the idea of one group using this new material, even though it kind of dented my ego that they would choose to do something other than what I had prepared. However, they were so excited about it they recruited members from other groups to join in. Initially the plan was for people to still meet with their original group and join the new material group as well. It didn't take long before people realized they didn't have time to commit two nights to small groups. Some joined the new material group and those who remained in their original small group did not have enough of a core so the two other groups stopped meeting all together. A fourth group was made up primarily of snow birds (retired folks who fly south for the winter to avoid the cold and snow) so they went on hiatus after Christmas. The new material only lasted about a dozen weeks and once it concluded none of the three groups impacted ever really got back on track. The snow bird group, which had even more people out of town than usual that year started to meet again in May, but ended at the first of June.

To give you some sense of the impact essentially losing these four groups for two-thirds of our year had on our program, you need to know that we started out in the fall with five groups. The following spring I received some criticism for both my "spotty" personal involvement in groups (did I mention I led the fifth group - the one that actually ran all year and followed the given schedule and material?) and for the lackluster impact of groups in general during the year. I felt like my leadership was questioned, my material was disregarded and my format was poo-pooed upon. On the one hand, you could argue I was in charge of small groups so I was responsible for keeping them on track and making sure they performed well all year. And I could have handled it if my group leaders didn't have enough support, if my material was ineffective, if my format was too erratic, if groups functioned exactly like I planned them to and failed miserably – Fine, that's on me and I'm okay with that. On the other hand, I felt like for the most part, nobody did what I had laid out for them to do and I was being graded on something I had no input on or control over.

I don't bring this all up to criticize the new material that was used. In fact I think it was okay stuff. I don't mention it to bemoan people not following _MY_ plan. I'm not telling you all this because I'm angry at any of the other group leaders or participants. I share this story for one reason: because it is a great example of what happens in ministry. I can clearly remember the Sunday morning when the leader I had recruited the previous August came up to me after service and said with a laugh, "By the way, did you hear that I killed Life Groups?" I had been told his group was switching to the new material, but he went on to explain how portions of the other groups were joining them and shutting down their own groups for the duration. It was the first I had heard anything about the plan and it was already a done deal.

One of the most frustrating things about being in ministry is you are held responsible for certain activities and the overall goals of the church, but you are not given much authority to make decisions or mandate certain activities be done a particular way. Often times someone else will make the plans and the decisions and then hand it over to you and say "Go out and make it work."

I don't particularly like to fail – I don't imagine many people do. But if I am going to fail I want at least one of two things to be true:
1. It was my plan which was carried out as designed but just didn't work
2. It was someone else's plan and I did my best with it, however in the end it is the one who designed the plan who is held accountable for it

Often what your minister will experience is the worst of both worlds. Either it was not his plan to begin with or his original plan was changed without his consent, yet in the end he is the one who has to answer the questions about why it didn't work out.

Perhaps it is like a football coach who notices the defence is playing several yards back off the ball leaving tons of room to run. He calls a handoff play and signals to the quarterback. The quarterback acknowledges the call, steps to the line, snaps the ball and instead of running the short play, throws it up deep into triple coverage. The ball is easily intercepted and run back for a touchdown by the opposing team. Instantly everyone in the stadium starts complaining to one another about the coaches' horrible play calling. I imagine there are times when your minister feels like that coach - either given a play book with plays he didn't design or calling plays he thinks will work only to have the players on the field choose to do something different. Then at the end of the day, he ends up being blasted on the call-in shows for the team's lack of success.

I remember the first all-nighter I had with my teens when I started in youth ministry. At the beginning of the night I gathered everyone together and went over all the rules. Basic stuff really. Boys don't go into the girl's room. Girls don't go into the boy's room. That kind of thing. Then I firmly and clearly stressed the number one rule for the night. No one, under any circumstances, may leave the building or go outside. Period. No exceptions. It was not more than an hour or two later when some of the girls came to me and said they were hearing strange noises outside and thought someone or something might be out there. I went out to look and sure enough I caught two sheepishly grinning teenage boys. Not entirely unexpected, I know. Here's the kicker though: I could have dealt with the boys and disciplined them for breaking the clearly stated rules easily enough. However, I quickly learned that they had ventured outside on this pranking mission not only with the permission of one of the volunteer chaperones who was there to help keep tabs on everyone, but in fact they were doing it all at *his* suggestion.

North American evangelical ministers are often the collateral damage of two prevailing ideologies. Depending on your particular denomination these principle may carry more or less weight. First is the doctrine of the priesthood of all believers. This one is especially strong in my fellowship. In a nutshell, this doctrine states we are all equal in Christ and as such there should be no elevation of any kind of the clergy. This, in the extreme, means that your minister should not have any more authority than anyone else in your congregation. The second dogma, especially prevalent in North America, is an idealist view of democracy. Naturally when applied to the church, this means everyone should get an equal vote and an equal say in how things are done. These philosophies combine in varying degrees to create an environment in your church where your minister is often only allowed to lead as long as he leads in the direction everyone is already going.

I remember in my first year or two of ministry – I was fresh out of college and was going to be all radical and innovative (or at least that's what I thought at the time). One week when I was the only person at our building, I unscrewed the pews from the floor. Instead of the standard two by two formation, I rearranged them in what I felt was a wonderful, fellowship enhancing U-shape. That's how I left things on Friday afternoon, but apparently Noah stopped by on Saturday because when I walked in on Sunday morning the pews were once again lined up two by two.

Of course that seems like a small thing and I lose absolutely no sleep over it these days, but I admit I lost a few winks over it at the time. Not so much because the event itself was a big deal, but the underlying reality was incredibly deflating. I knew how our pews were arranged wasn't going to be the make it or break it factor in the health of our congregation or our ability to reach out to our community. But my young, idealistic self had just got a two-by-four upside the head and I came to with the realization that any of my plans, goals or strategies could be completely undone, literally overnight, if someone in my church thought there was a better way – or simply didn't like my way.

I recall in that same congregation there was one of the sweetest and most godly older women you are ever bound to meet. This particular lady had a very special gift. She had a knack for suggesting you should do something in a way that you absolutely couldn't say no. She was the grandmother-Godfather – regularly making me an offer I couldn't refuse! This family wanted someone to come spend time with their kids; this woman needed help cleaning out her basement; Meals on Wheels needed people to deliver lunches – whatever it happened to be, she would come up to me, tell me all about whatever it was she thought needed to be done and then, as I stood there like a deer in the headlights – knowing exactly what was coming but unable to get out the way, she would say, "Oh, well, you could do that, couldn't you?" What do you say to that? You say, "Yeah, I guess I could."

And I'm not complaining. She was a wonderful woman and most of the stuff she got me to do was worthwhile. As a young minister starting out, it was good to get a broad experience of things. But there have been many other times when I have been outright commanded or more subtly 'voluntold' to take on certain projects I loathed. Sometimes it was a project I knew was doomed to fail due to poor design, but I had to carry it all out (according to design) anyway. Sometimes the activity wasn't inherently bad, but just really wasn't in the mandate of my particular ministry portfolio. Which meant I had to take time away from the things I was supposed to be doing to do this other thing or, more likely, try and make time to do both. Sometimes I was simply not gifted at, qualified for or comfortable with the task. In all these cases as a minister I can, and on some occasions probably should, go ahead, grit my teeth, make like a Nike shoe and just do it. And I'm okay with that, but I also know it's going to take something out of me.

FOR MINISTERS ONLY:

Getting roped into doing stuff you'd rather not do just kind of goes with the territory. As much as possible, make your peace with it and know sometimes this is just part of the job. However, there are occasions when it is perfectly acceptable and I would argue the 'right thing to do' for you to say, "I'm sorry, but I really can't help you out with that this time round."

Ministry can be like that at times and it can be a frustrating thing. It's much like trying to drive a car without any direct control over the wheel (or the gas, the brake, the indicator, the wipers, the headlights or the radio). Whether it's your own plans being hijacked or being given a project or strategy not of your own design you have to somehow make work – over time it can drain the zest right out of you.

WHAT MIGHT HELP?

Again, I think some of the issues are inherent to the structures and systems of our churches in general. And that doesn't necessarily mean those structures or systems are bad, but there are some inevitable side effects. The greatest thing you can do may be to simply increase awareness and sensitivity to this concern in both yourself and others in your congregation. As far as more tangible action steps, you might consider starting with some of the following:

- *Stand up for your minister.* Support his ideas and plans. Be his cheerleader. Encourage others to get "on board" and "buy in" to his strategies and programs. Most importantly lead by example in this regard.
- *Keep others on board.* When you sense someone may be inadvertently derailing things gently suggest giving the minister's strategy a fair chance to work first or suggest the person should look for an opportunity to pursue their idea in a way that will not inhibit or jeopardize what your minister is already trying to accomplish.
- *Get him off the hook.* Encourage people to find sources of man power for their ministry ideas in someone other than the minister. Your minister simply does not have the time

and energy to be involved in everything your church is actively doing. Nor is he always the most suited or qualified to do so. Between you and me, if your minister can be involved with every ministry and attend every activity your church has going on – your church doesn't have enough going on.

- **Back him up.** Let your minister know you're behind him. When you can't be involved physically, let him know you support the idea. When you see him doing his best to make something good out of a bad plan he's been handed, encourage him in his efforts and join in if you can. Just knowing someone else recognizes the situation will take a huge weight off his shoulders.

REASON #3

Fishbowls

In my first year of ministry I was preaching at a little church in a small town – and I mean small. The population of our tiny community was between 500 – 700 depending on who you talked to and how big they drew the circle. Our church had between 25 and 35 people on an average Sunday and almost none of them lived in the actual town where our building was located. Most lived on farms or in other towns 10 to 45 minutes away. My not-yet-wife was still attending college about 800 miles away so I was living on my own. About twenty minutes away was our denomination's church camp. That summer there were several counsellors at the camp whom I knew and was friends with. One weekend, instead of driving all the way home on Friday evening just to drive all the way back on Sunday morning, a couple of the counsellors decided to just stay at the camp for the weekend and relax. I had been out to the camp earlier that week and made plans to meet up with them on Friday night. So that's what we did.

Friday evening, after all the kids had been picked up and the camp had been cleaned up, they drove into town and we went out to grab some supper. Like I said, it was a small town so there was really only one place to eat that was open late. These days in the city we'd call it a sports bar, back then in that town it was just called "The Bar". It wasn't anything fancy but they did serve both a bison burger and a bear burger, which disappointingly was just a really big beef burger. We hung out there for a while ate our burgers and drank our - for the record - completely non-alcoholic colas. Then we went back to my place to watch a movie. This is what twenty year olds do right? By the time the movie was done and my friends headed back to the camp for the night it was quite late - probably midnight or so. It was a fun night and rather refreshing for me as I didn't have a lot of peers who lived nearby.

Sunday morning came around and after service one of our church leaders took me aside and had a little chat with me. Oh, by the way, did I mention both of my friends from camp happened to be female? I didn't think much of it at the time, but apparently that was significant. The leader went on to suggest, gently but firmly, it was not appropriate for a single man to have two girls at his place into the wee hours of the night and I would be wise not to repeat Friday's agenda again.

To give full credit to the church leader who chatted with me: First, they actually came and talked to me about it in a kind and friendly way. Second, they expressed complete trust in me that nothing inappropriate had happened. The thought had never even crossed my mind. I was in a committed relationship with my future wife and one of the girls was dating a good friend of mine. We were just friends hanging out and watching a movie.

Perhaps the most interesting part of this story is, as I mentioned, almost none of my church members actually lived in town. Which means it was not one of my members who observed this apparent indiscretion. No, in fact it was one of my neighbors who then talked to someone who talked to someone in my church. And thus I got the "it just doesn't look very good for the minister to ..." conversation. Looking back I can sort of see the issue and I have no doubt these things are quickly amplified in a small town environment where everyone knows everyone else's business. But it does serve to illustrate **Reason #3** really well.

Your minister - and their spouse and their kids - live in a fishbowl. They are always being watched. Always being observed. Always being judged and graded. In some ways it seems really unfair – especially when some church members insist on holding their ministers accountable to a standard they themselves rarely seem to meet. In other ways it's merely an unavoidable occupational hazard. The two questions I regularly get asked when I meet someone are: "What do you do?" Which is usually followed up with "Oh, for what church?" And from that moment on, everything I say and do is directly linked back to my church, my profession, Christians in general and God Himself.

To some extent you could argue every Christian should be mindful of the impression they are giving to others by their words and actions and I would agree with you. However, most regular Christians don't get outted like ministers do and somehow there seems to be the perspective – even among non-Christians – that ministers should be held to a higher standard of conduct. Consider this:

- My neighbors know I am a minister and therefore every dealing I have with them and even what they observe of me with my family or out in my yard is viewed through that lens.
- When I am on sports teams, my teammates know I am a minister, therefore if I curse, lose my temper, play chippy or drink beer after the game they notice.
- My kid's friend's parents know I'm a minister and therefore how my marriage is, how my home is run and how my kids behave are all associated with ministers, church and Christians
- Even the person who cuts my hair knows I'm a minister and which church I work at! So do the waitresses at a couple of the restaurants near our building!

Every time I act in what is perceived as the wrong way; every time I say something deemed inappropriate; every time I laugh at a joke considered to be too crass every time I watch a movie deemed by someone to be too violent or to have too much language in it; every time I say or do anything it is

72

filtered through people's expectation of a minister. Other Christians can fly under the radar. They can get away with things without people thinking twice about it. They can have relationships with people without those people even knowing that they are, in fact, Christians.

FOR MINISTERS ONLY:

The upside of this reality is it creates many great opportunities. Some of your best conversations will be with people you meet at the gym, the motor speedway or pottery class. When people know you're in ministry, even though they may initially become more tentative around you, when they need someone to talk to about the really important stuff in life you may very well be at the top of their list. This past Sunday I had a five minute conversation with the barista at my local Starbucks about how sometimes life is not fair. The conversation started when he asked me, "What is your sermon on today?" This discussion would have never occurred if he didn't know I was a minister.

Consider this: which of your neighbors, co-workers, teammates, kid's friend's parents, barbers, waiters or any other person you have regular contact with know that you are a Christian and directly associate your actions with your professed faith? For your minister, it's pretty much everyone.

It all amounts to a lot of pressure. A lot of stress. It makes your minister feel like he's always got to be 'on'. He's got to be at the top of his game. He has to constantly assess and reassess every action and word, anticipate how people will view it and extrapolate how it will impact their opinion of church, Christianity and God. It can be exhausting.

SIDENOTE Several weeks ago one of the baristas at my local Starbucks discovered I am a minister. Today was the first day I crossed paths with him on a Sunday morning. After the regular chit chat he asked me if I was doing the service today. The way he asked indicated to me he hasn't had a lot of experience with churches in the past. As I walked out to my car, mochaccino in hand, I pondered my wardrobe which today was nice but casual. Perhaps the barista thought my church must be pretty hip and cool if the minister wears jeans to church. Maybe he was surprised that I wasn't decked out in a three piece suit. Or it could be he was thinking "I guess it doesn't matter what you wear under your robes." I don't actually wear robes, but the point is what you do might be viewed as a reflection on you or perhaps your faith. What your minister does is often considered to be a reflection on your entire church and sometimes Christianity as a whole.

And it's not just his evangelistic witness he's trying to preserve, it's also his job, his livelihood and his ability to provide for his family! As much as we all love each other in the church, every minister lives with the reality that if there ever comes a time when the people in his congregation are not satisfied with his lifestyle, his family, his teaching or his productivity he could very quickly find himself looking through the help wanted section. You know how challenging living out your faith in a consistent Christ-like manner can be. Now imagine if your career and your income depended on it! And in a small denomination like mine, it doesn't take long at all for word to spread to all your potential future congregations about why you just got let go from your current congregation. So unless your minister's spouse makes a boatload of money and he's just doing this church thing for the fun of it, there is a cartoon sized anvil of weight upon your minister to *always* meet *everyone's* expectations.

Which brings us to another phenomenon unique to ministry. There are extremely few times, around extremely few people I can take off my metaphorical minister's hat. I can't do it around church people. I can't do it around non-church people who know I am a minister. I can really only clock out when I am around close family and friends or complete strangers. Even around complete strangers I have to make sure they don't know anyone from my church. That's not to say I want to go wild in Vegas or chug a bottle of Tequila, I just need a moment to relax and just be Mike, (we'll talk more about that when we get to **Reason #7**).

I love the members of our church and I enjoy hanging out with many of them. But I can never really just hang out with any of them just as buds, because in the back of their minds I will always be their minister. And whenever I go to do my 'minister' duties, what I did while we were hanging out will be in the back of their heads too. It reminds me of having a parent chaperone you on a date. Sure you can go to the movie and drink milkshakes afterwards, but you're always looking over your shoulder, or have someone else looking over *your* shoulder. You know you're being watched and judged and assessed and graded. Especially if it's *your date's parent* chaperoning you. So, you can go out and do stuff and have fun, but you're never really relaxed or free to just be yourself. Even on those occasions when no one is actually watching, your minister's Spidy-sense is so used to being on high alert he _feels_ as though he's still under the microscope. I know it sounds a little narcissistic, but this is the way past experiences have programed many minsters to function.

For your minister, this can be exhausting and draining. Worse yet, if it happens consistently enough for long enough, your minister might actually struggle with a bigger problem. You've likely heard stories or watched movies about an undercover cop who maintains her alter ego persona for so long that she actually begins to be that person. The same thing can happen to your minister, only in reverse. If your minister feels like he is always on and never has any down time to just be himself (not the preacher) he may subtly slip into a place where he starts to feel like his minister persona is simply just that. Without sufficient time with the minister hat off and the fishbowl curtains drawn your minister will not have the energy to authentically be that person and therefore out of pure necessity, knowing how much is riding on all this, he is forced to merely try and keep up appearances. Over the course of time, your minister's actions will become less genuine and more façade. This is not by design or desire it is simply the way things go. He simply does not have enough energy to keep up with the demands of all the watching eyes all the time. The worst-case scenario is that he will wake up one morning and realize that ministry is just a persona for him and not really who he is anymore. If something doesn't change for him quickly it won't be long before he either resigns or gets himself into some kind of moral difficulty that forces him to step away from ministry altogether.

SIDENOTE: In my experience a very high percentage of ministers are also, somewhat ironically, introverts. Extroverts gain energy from being with people and lose energy from being alone. Introverts are the exact opposite: their energy is drained when they are interacting with people and restored by time alone. Apply that principle to the fishbowl effect and you can see how the constant direct or indirect interaction with the people around them can quickly zap all of the fuel out of their tank.

This morning (Sunday) I walked out to my car and my neighbor was working in her yard. We exchanged a couple quick "Hi! How are ya?"s and then she gave me a wave and said, "Have a good day at work." That seems to be a perfect example of what this chapter is talking about. Not only does it affirm the assertion everyone I have regular contact with is aware I am a minister and views everything I do through the lens of that knowledge, but it also illustrates the reality that you go to church on Sundays, but your minister goes to work.

WHAT MIGHT HELP?

As with the previous two reasons the fishbowl effect may just be part and parcel to the whole ministry experience. There may be very little that you or your minister can do to change that reality. Perhaps the best thing that we can hope to do is minimize the effect that it has on your minister and counteract those effects as best we can. Here are a few simple suggestions that might help:

- **Cut your minister some slack**. Acknowledge the fact he's a regular Christian just like you. And just like you don't always get it right or aren't always at your best, he may not be either. Let him know you don't expect him to be. Don't gasp in shock when he's not. Protect him from others who are overly critical - we'll talk about that more when we get to **Reason #4**.

- **Ensure your minister gets enough downtime**. We will discuss this at length in **Reason #7**, but for now, both allow and encourage your minister to find opportunities where he can just be himself. Where he is not "on the job." Make sure he and his family have opportunities to get out of the fishbowl and just be a husband; a wife; a man; a woman; a kid; a father; a son; a mother; a daughter – regular, ordinary, everyday people.

REASON #4
Critics

I once tried to illustrate the dichotomy between the world's view of love and God's view. I had someone prep two PowerPoint slideshows: one with photos of what the world sees as love and one with photos of what God sees love as. I set both presentations to music. For the God slideshow I picked some churchy song – I honestly can't even remember what it was. For worldly love it didn't make sense to me to use a worship song, so I used a portion of *Crazy Little Thing Called Love*. That was on September 13, 2009. It was in my first year at that congregation and coincidentally the day of my 12th wedding anniversary. Later in the week I got a call from a disgruntled member chastising me for how inappropriate my song selection was. At the time I thought, "It was supposed to be inappropriate, that was the point – to illustrate the contrast between ... oh well, never mind." *I was completely slayed by that phone call.* I was so crushed I deleted the audio file from my computer. It's been almost five years and just a couple weeks ago was the first time I could hear that song on the radio and not feel sick to my stomach, but I still feel some remnant of the criticism (and am compelled to change the station when it comes on). I kid you not, I kind of feel like I need to take a break from writing after telling the story to you. That's how devastating harsh criticism can be to your minister.

Wherever you work, you may have a supervisor or manager. You might even have a few layers of bosses to deal with and conform to. Your minister is open to criticism and evaluation by everyone who walks through the doors of your church. Before I get to the members of your church, consider first those who aren't regular attenders.

Statistics tell us there are certain criteria on which visitors based their decision to return or not to return to your church. Elements like friendliness, worship style and kids classes are certainly among the top of the list. Also near or at the top of the list is people's reaction to your minister. In most churches the sermon portion of the morning makes up close to half of the worship time, so no one wants to go to a church with a boring preacher. People are looking for a preacher who can be interesting, entertaining, encouraging and challenging – but not too challenging. They want someone who can make the Bible make sense to them and help them draw practical applications to everyday life. And if I can't do that for you the first Sunday you visit my church odds are greatly diminished we will ever see you again. But it's not just my speaking style on trial here. I need to come across as friendly, warm, welcoming, concerned, well-informed and relatable. On any Sunday I can't pull all that off there is a chance those who are visiting for the first time will not come back. Whether visitors state their criticism verbally or state it by simply not returning, you can be certain your minister gets the message loud and clear.

I recall one occasion when my wife was criticized for not shaking the hand of a visitor when they first walked into the building. It was clearly expressed to her the expectation of the minister's wife was to greet all visitors who came to our church. The irony of the situation was the person who was put out by this inadvertent snub was a relative of someone at our church and almost certainly had been at our church more Sundays as a visitor than my wife had attended as a member at that point in time.

The reality of your minister's job leaves him open to criticism and second-guessing by anyone who comes to your church. Sometimes the criticism comes discretely, sometimes publically and sometimes passive-aggressively. Sometimes it comes subversively as the grouser who never speaks to your minister directly but instead criticizes him to everyone else when he is not around. Over the years I have received criticism for several different things. Let me give you some of my favorite examples:

- My sermon introductions are too long.
- My sermons are too short – I know it's hard to believe but I'm dead serious.
- I wasn't connecting well enough with some of the kids in my youth group.
- I don't wear a tie often enough.
- I'm not spending enough time at the office.
- I was once criticized for walking to work. (I know it sounds strange but the real beef was people didn't know if I was at the office if my car wasn't parked in front of the building).
- On one occasion I was doing a sermon series on knowing our identity – who we are in Christ – and I showed a movie clip to illustrate a sermon point (something we do at our church from time to time). In the clip two people are sitting calmly in a diner and one of the characters says, "*I can tell you the license plate number of all six cars outside. I can tell you that our waitress is left handed and the guy sitting at the bar weighs 215 pounds and knows how to handle himself. I know the best place to look*

for a gun is in the cab of the grey truck outside. And at this altitude I can run flat out for half a mile before my hands start shaking. How can I know all that and not know who I am?" Later, I had one church member complain because I was showing violent movies in church.

- I do not visit or call certain people often enough.
- I do not give an official invitation at the end of service every week.
- My schedule for small groups requires people to meet too often, not enough, or too inconsistently.

SIDENOTE Remember the challenge of being a one car family I described at the start of this book? I know of ministers who have caught significant flack for very similar scenarios, either for not showing up early enough or not bringing their family with them to every church activity.

The list could go on but I don't want to gripe. My goal here is not to complain about the people who have criticized me over the past 20 years but my hope is to help you see some of the things your minister has to deal with and the effect it has on him. Often as a minister tries to achieve the goals set out for him, there are those who have a better idea of how to do it or a different way to accomplish it or have another more important priority.

Not to mention in this day of smartphones and tablets every time a minister opens his mouth there is a fury of feverish fingers tap, tap, tapping, googling, Wikipediaing and scouring the internet to check, crosscheck and double check what he says. I'm not suggesting a minister should be able to say whatever he wants whether it's true or not. However, I always know if I accidentally misquote a statistic, misstate a fact or misspell something on a handout immediately following service there will be someone there to point it out to me. The people in my church tend to be fairly gracious and kind, but not every minister is so lucky.

Everyone in your church has an opinion about what your minister should be doing and how he should be doing it. It can become very frustrating for your minister when every idea he puts forward, every program he structures, every suggestion he makes is met with someone else's opinion of a better way to do it. This is especially true because while your minister has a view of the broad picture of the church and has his finger on the pulse of many different aspects of your congregation, those who are leveling the criticism and making the suggestions often do not. Therefore their alternate suggestions may make sense in regard to one particular area, however it may also cause a lot of other problems and frustrations in other areas that they are unaware of.

SIDENOTE: Think back to the story I told you about small groups in Reason #2. The new material wasn't bad, in some ways it was a good idea. The problem was in the bigger picture: using that material, at that time, in that way may have done more harm than help in the grand scheme of things.

I remember in my early days as a youth minister trying to settle on the best night to hold youth activities. Each student and their parent had a different night that worked best for them. I had to choose a night that worked best for the most people knowing full well there would be some people who would not like my choice and may not be able to attend. I have had to make dozens or even hundreds of similar decisions over my ministry career. Sometimes they are accepted with gracious understanding and sometimes I have been nailed to the wall for them.

I think every congregation has its resident critics. These are the folks who are regularly and easily offended. They have a nose like an old boxer – permanently out of joint. These are the people who call the minister on Monday morning or send anonymous notes in the mail. These are the ones who generally have a sour disposition and seem intent on being unhappy regardless of the circumstances. You are almost certainly *not* one of these people. If you were you would have used this book for kindling a long time ago or probably never even bought it in the first place (Unless you thought this book might give you some ideas on how to finally push your minister over the edge). So please understand this chapter isn't targeted at you. But also understand these people's criticism is usually targeted at your minister. Right or wrong, it is usually the minister who is held responsible first and foremost for the majority of things occurring within your congregation. The assumption is your minister is the one who has initiated the activity, was pushing for things to go a certain direction or should have stepped in to prevent it. The effect of this reality impacts your minister in two ways:

The first impact on your minister is the toll the criticism itself takes upon him. Nobody likes to be criticized. Nobody likes to have their work judged or poo-pooed upon. No one likes to bear the brunt of someone else's wrath. Generally speaking we all want to be liked by others. We all want others to think we're a pretty decent person. We all want our ideas to be held up as brilliant not shot down as idiotic. So when someone levels criticism at us it hurts - particularly when that criticism is offered with venom. To make matters worse, from your minister's point of view, this harsh criticism he is receiving is coming from someone whom he is trying to love, trying to help and trying to serve. It is coming from someone who he understood to be his brother or sister in Christ. Someone he believed was looking out for *his* best interests. Someone he had counted on to be his friend not his enemy. In some ways, when people you've invested so much love and care into turn on you it is similar, in many ways, to how a parent feels when their child lashes out with barbs like "I hate you!" or "You're mean!" or "I wish you weren't my dad!"

I have already described for you the impact criticism has had on me at times - even over *crazy little things*. And I suppose you could argue I need to toughen up. I need to grow a thicker skin. I need to allow those comments to be like water off a duck's back to me. And perhaps this is true, at least to a degree. Nonetheless you need to be aware of how criticism impacts your minister. Even if it's not coming from you it is likely coming from someone. As optimistic as your minister might be, every blow of criticism either deflates his balloon of enthusiasm a little or pops it altogether. Given time, his enthusiasm can be rebuilt, but if it takes too many hits in close succession there may be no hope for recovery.

That's not to say that all ministers are dainty little souls needing to be handled with kid gloves. There are times when constructive criticism is valuable – even needed. But effective and positive criticism can only come when:

1. A loving and healthy relationship between the one offering suggestions and the minister has already been firmly established, where the minister has no doubt in his mind the person providing the constructive criticism wants nothing but the best for the minister and offers

his words in complete and utter love. Not everyone in your congregation fits this description, in fact, most of the people in your congregation will not fit this description. You may be one of those people, but if you are not (or you're not sure if you are) share your thoughts with someone who is and allow them to discern whether or not and how to share those concerns with your minister.

2. The person offering the criticism is committed to working together with the minister to find a positive and workable solution or alternative to the issue being criticized. Nothing is more frustrating and irritating than for someone to say, "The way you are doing things really sucks, but don't ask me to come up with a better alternative or help you implement a better plan."

However, critics in your church are impacting your minister in a way that might be even more detrimental than the initial sucker punch to the emotional gut. When your minister is attacked by critics often enough, there is a residual effect that continues to impact his ministry effectiveness long after the comments have passed. The critic's lambasting can do several things to your minister. Here is how the process works:

A. The critic's comment can rob your minister of his enthusiasm for the work he is doing. It is hard to be excited about doing a job you know you are going to get criticized for. If you knew your boss was going to call you into his office and chew you out every Monday morning, you certainly wouldn't be very excited about going to work, would you?

B. Your minister becomes gun shy. He begins to shy away from anything he thinks may invoke criticism from someone in his congregation. He is tired of getting hammered for showing movie clips in his sermon so he stops showing movie clips. He is tired of being criticized for how small groups are run so he gives up on structuring small groups. He's tired of being criticized for not having a visible presence at the office enough so he buys a cheap used car, parks it at the office all the time and spends his days at Starbucks. The point is he stops trying new things. He stops innovating. He stops thinking out-of-the-box. He sticks to what is safe, the things that are least likely to rock the boat, make waves or land him in the splash zone. Not only is this a bad thing for your minister but it is also a detriment to your congregation.

C. The last phase of the progression is your minister becomes cynical. He starts to think thoughts like:

- "Why should I bother even coming up with an idea if it's just going to get shot down anyways?"
- "What's the use of trying something new if all I'm going to get is complaints?"

- "Here I am trying to help these people and all they do is hammer me for it. What sense does that make?"

SIDENOTE This reinforces the critic's belief that criticism is an effective way to get what they want. If someone criticizes your minister for doing something they don't like and the minister stops doing that thing then every time in the future when the minister does something they don't like they will attack without reservation having full confidence that their criticism will persuade the minister to alter his behavior to what they find acceptable. Every time this method is successful it emboldens the critics in your church to attack more often and ferociously over less and less important issues.

I likely don't need to tell you having a minister who has begun thinking this way is not good for anyone. His effectiveness in leading the congregation will be greatly diminished and he may even find himself on the side of those who are rejecting ideas out of hand because his experience has taught him they won't fly anyway. When your minister gets to this point, it is not a long leap between cynical and "Why am I even doing this anymore? Maybe it's time to do something else."

WHAT MIGHT HELP?

Finally!! An issue I can say something other than, "It's just kind of the nature of the beast. It comes with the territory. It's just part of the job." On this count I can say unequivocally, "This is not the way it has to be. This is not the way it should be. This is not the way you should let it stay." In a religion whose core tenets are love and grace (among others) there is absolutely no way in heaven your minister should be subject to destructive criticism. There is no way any Christian should participate in such things. There is no way Christians should condone these actions. There is no way Christians should permit these things to happen. If you're interested in weeding these critics out of your congregation or at the very least protecting your minister from them, here's a few suggestions of some potential starting points:

- **Don't be critical.** It seems like it goes without saying but I've said it anyways just to make sure. Unless *your minister* feels like you have the kind of relationship with him that makes criticism appropriate: don't do it. If you have concerns talk to someone in your congregation who does have the relationship with your minister to address them (preferably one of your church leaders).
- **Don't be nit-picky.** Don't hassle your minister over the little details that could really be done a number of different ways all of which are equally fine. It may not seem like a big thing

to you but consider how you would feel if you had an idea and everyone in the congregation constantly came up and offered you their ideas for tweaks and improvements and alterations.

- **Don't allow it.** If you hear of or overhear somebody criticizing your minister *shut it down*. Tell the person you are talking to it is not appropriate. Defend your minister's choices and decisions or at the very least defend his intentions. If the person you are talking to still will not let it go, redirect them to your church leaders. Hopefully you are not already talking to one of your church leaders.

- **Pay attention**. Keep an eye on your minister. Get to know his moods a little. Try to discern when he is up and when he is down. When that encouragement balloon is full and when it is empty. Admittedly, many of us try very hard to hide things and make you think we are up all the time. That's our problem and we need to work on it. When you are unable to intercept a critic's attack, at least do what you can to offset it with encouragement and positive affirmation.

Even as I write these words I'm worried that someone will read them and criticize me for what I've said. I am concerned someone out there will say all sorts of nasty things about me because of what I've written. What if someone comes along and says all that stuff is just garbage, none of it is real? What if I get written up in some journal or magazine that tells all its readers I don't have the first clue of what I'm talking about? What if some other dude comes along and writes a book talking about how all the stuff in my book is pure malarkey? Hmm, I wonder if I can charge royalties on every quote he takes from this book? Your minister has more than enough things to do and more than enough stress to deal with. The last thing he needs is a slew of critics heckling him from the peanut gallery. Between you and me it's the last thing your church needs too.

FOR MINISTERS ONLY:
You are not infallible. There are times when you will benefit greatly from a little constructive criticism. It is your responsibility to cultivate relationships with individuals in your church so they will be in a position to provide you with constructive criticism when it is needed. These people help serve as a barometer for you and assist you in knowing which criticisms to consider seriously and which ones to block out, ignore, erase or burn and forget.

REASON #5
Spinning Plates

Have you ever been to the circus and seen one of those guys spinning four, five, six plates at a time? No, me neither. I don't even know if the circus actually has those. Do you? Whether or not you've actually seen one or not almost everyone is familiar with the image. There is a man frantically going from one stick to the next to the next. Give plate number one a couple spins to keep its velocity up then quickly move to plate number two and so on and so on. Those who are really good at it can keep all the plates spinning and continue to cycle through the line before any plate slows down enough that it topples off the stick and crashes to the floor. I think a lot of people might select this imagery to illustrate their job. I think your minister is one of those people.

One of the realities of ministry, especially in single or small staff churches, is the minister must be able to multitask. He is required to handle a variety of different chores on any given day. He must possess the ability to be working on one thing, be interrupted to do another thing, move on to complete a third thing before eventually getting back to continue working on the first thing. That's how most of my days go anyway. Whether it is phone calls, emails, meter readers, colleagues, appointments, drop by visitors or a number of other things, my day is often interrupted and disjointed. Over the years I've learned various skills and techniques to help me balance all the various needs that come up on a day-to-day basis. I'm still learning.

But it's more than just disruptions. On any given day your minister may be required to work on several different projects simultaneously. He has a sermon to prep for Sunday, a class to prep for Wednesday night, information to disperse to small group leaders, next week's service project to finalize, November's workshop to organize, a member to visit in the hospital, a colleague to assist or mentor, an elders meeting to prepare for, a special activity to plan and a handful of other things. If he plans his day well and transitions from one thing to the next smoothly, he can accomplish a lot. On other days everything takes far longer than he expected it would and progress comes much slower than he would like.

Again other jobs may not be very different and I think, generally speaking, most ministers are happy to accept this fact. But here's where things get more complicated: a lot of ministers end up spinning plates they were not adequately trained for nor do they have a passion for or interest in. There are a lot of things that for one reason or another have landed on your minister's desk.
- They may be there because he has taken them on himself.

- They may be there because the previous minister had taken it upon himself.
- They may be there by default because the minister is simply the most pragmatic option given his regular office hours at the church building.
- They may be there because they are very important, but your minister has been unable to find someone else who can adequately complete the task – reliably and on time – and is willing to do so.
- They may be there because someone else in the congregation has decided that this is something the minister should be doing and therefore dropped it in his lap.

In many cases, to legitimately complete the tasks assigned, your minister should have a degree in psychology, marketing, social work, IT, accounting, business management, tax law, human resources, administration, basic carpentry/plumbing, public relations, event planning, leadership training and probably something Bibley wouldn't hurt either. Most of the churches today, even the smaller ones, have acquired a vast array of organizational needs. A minister often finds himself not merely ministering to people but running the organization on a day-to-day basis which is equivalent to operating a small, or not so small, business. At some churches the minister's duties may include making copies, preaching sermons, running programs, changing light bulbs, organizing small groups, mowing the lawn, hospital visitation, managing building projects, creating publications and study materials, putting salt on the sidewalks to melt the ice, producing bulletins and maintain church websites, dealing with administration needs, local outreach, planning Christmas pageants, having the building sign replaced, supervising other staff, overseeing thousands of dollars in missions funds, various staff, elder, committee meetings and a host of other responsibilities. As a result many ministers are left feeling like they have more plates to spin than they can possibly keep up with and several of those plates have absolutely nothing to do with the reason they got into ministry in the first place.

The time and effort it takes to keep the wheels turning and lights on at your church is truly staggering. The bigger the church, the more programs, the more work it takes just to keep things spinning round. I can't speak for your minister, but my hunch is if you ask him he will tell you he didn't get into ministry to do administration or management. If I had to guess, I'd say he got into ministry to impact people's lives for the glory of God. But the reality is your minister ends up doing a whole bunch of stuff other than the stuff that drew him to ministry originally.

I have talked to many ministers about this issue and most come to the same conclusion: *I spend so much time operating the church and running programs I barely have any time left over for ministry. So much of my schedule is eaten up just doing the stuff I have to do to get through the week there is hardly any room for anything other than what has to get done before Sunday.* I know this certainly epitomizes many of my weeks. This modern reality can have a double impact on your minister.

FOR MINISTERS ONLY:
Despite the crazy and busy schedule you will inevitably have at times, you should always be searching for new ways and methods to use your time more efficiently. Anything you can do to better manage your time or squeeze out more productivity from your work hours will be a huge advantage to both you and your congregation. There are numerous books and resources that can help you in this endeavor but in the end you'll need to experiment and find out what works best for you. Not only will this help you get more accomplished, but it will help you be a better steward of the gifts and opportunities God has given you.

First, and most obviously, it can make your minister extremely busy. According to the statistics, the average minister works more than 50 hours a week. As you'll read in later chapters tracking hours for ministers is a very complicated endeavor – and is one, I might say, I'm not very keen on – but I would venture to say the number of hours logged by many ministers could be significantly higher depending on the list of activities you counted as work time. I'm sure, like in any profession, there are some in ministry who have – how shall we say it – a less vigorous regiment when it comes to their work schedule. However my experience with the vast majority of ministers I have met and known is they are putting in far more hours than they technically need to or in some cases should. Some of this comes from elevated expectations – whether from the congregation or the minister himself. However, I am convinced much of it comes simply from the fact that ministers feel they must put in that many hours just to get done what they need to get done. In fact, I would venture to guess most ministers would say even with extended hours they fail to accomplish as much as they feel they should most weeks.

On the one hand we can admire the dedication of these people who are willing to give so much extra for the sake of the kingdom, on the other hand there are some undeniable results that come from logging these kinds of hours on a consistent basis. The most visible by-product of this overloaded work week is the gradual exhaustion and eventual burnout of your minister. No one can keep up that kind of pace indefinitely, especially in the people oriented, highly relational, emotionally draining, eternal implication filled field of ministry. We'll talk a lot more about this when we get to **Reason #7**.

The other undeniable effect of logging so many hours of work is the toll it takes on your family. Whether you're a minister, an engineer, an IT specialist or a retail cashier the evidence is overwhelming and undeniable when you put in an excessive amount of time at your place of work your family suffers. When added to all the other complications that ministry brings to family life, clocking huge hours away from home can be disastrous for your marriage and your kids. I'm guessing if you've been in church for very long at all you can readily think of an example – or two or three – where a minister's family life has struggled and suffered. Odds are all the time spent trying to keep all the plates spinning was a significant factor.

SIDENOTE   In my opinion, speaking now as a PK (preacher's kid) who by God's grace and my parent's determination survived relatively unscathed, this is scandalous.   The church should be setting the benchmark in our society for valuing and caring for the family life of its employees.   Instead, in many cases, the church demands and requires so much of its employees and treats them in such a way that their families are permanently scarred or destroyed.   That can't be right.

The second impact of having too many plates to spin is that the bulk of your minister's time will be eaten up spinning the plates not related to his gifts and passions. I experienced a shocking and undeniable change when I made the shift from youth ministry to a lead minister position. As a youth minister life was great. All I had to worry about was doing ministry with my teens. The vast majority of my work was hands-on, frontline ministry. Not only did it mesh well with my passions at the time, but it gave me countless opportunities to unleash my creative side. When I switched roles all that changed. All of those things I never had to worry about as a youth minister because they were my lead minister's problem were now piled on *my* desk. Operational and organizational needs abounded. I found myself spending more and more time operating and managing the church leaving less and less time for actual ministry. I found the areas where my skills were strongest and my passions burned brightest tended to be the things I rarely had time to get to. Although I still had creative ideas, only occasionally did I have time to indulge them. Moreover, I found some of the ministry activities I should have been enjoying often became more frustration than pleasure because I simply didn't have enough time to do them as well as I desired. So I was left with the worst of all worlds:

- I was spending a lot of my time doing things I had little interest in or desire to do
- I rarely had opportunities to engage in areas of ministry where my gifts were strongest and I derived the most joy
- Even the areas of ministry where I was gifted and did have a passion, I didn't have enough time to complete projects to the level of my satisfaction and therefore I ended up being frustrated with the results feeling like opportunities had been wasted

A dear friend and colleague of mine once told me "Burnout comes not from overwork but from under-meaning." This is a statement I would endorse wholeheartedly. Burn out comes from lack of purpose. It comes from spending too little of your time doing things that really stoke your fire. Exhaustion comes from overwork, but burnout comes from under meaning – having too many plates to spin creates both of these issues for your minister. Many ministers have cashed in their clerical chips because they got tired of spinning plates that didn't matter to them while the plates they truly cherished got squeezed out of their schedule. When this happens a minister wakes up one morning and says to himself, "This is not what I signed up for. This is not why I got into ministry. What am I really accomplishing here anyways? I never wanted to be an Operational Manager, I wanted to be a Minister. I could do more true ministry and care for my family better if I left ministry altogether and just got a regular job."

Some of you are likely thinking to yourself, "Hey, I have a 'regular' job. I have to put in long hours. I get assigned tasks I'd rather not have to do. Parts of my job don't exactly float my boat either, you know." You may never get paid for your overtime hours. You may have to be on call virtually at any time of any day. You may regularly get brought in on weekends or evenings. That all may very well be the case and if it is I hope that things change for you. If I could change it for you I would most happily do so. But consider this: Would you change these aspects of your job if you could? I assume you answered "Well, duh. Yeah!" In which case I'd suggest if the only reason you think your minister should have to function in undesirable work conditions is because your employer makes you do it, I'm not sure that's really the most God-pleasing perspective to have. If nothing else, from a purely pragmatic point of view, you want your church to get the most bang for its buck out of your minister don't you? In that case, it is in your own best interests to put him in a position here he can invest most of his time in things he is most passionate about and most gifted at.

SIDENOTE If you recall the statistics listed at the beginning of this book, an alarmingly high percentage of ministers say they don't have time for reading their Bibles other than in preparation for a class or sermon. Many ministers also find time for inspirational and encouraging reading, prayer, devotional or meditation time is extremely rare if it exists at all. Although this seems like an enormous paradox, the reality is there are numerous plates that are far more urgent and demanding than these spiritually nourishing activities. When push comes to shove in your minister's schedule, the "have to get done" items will quickly squeeze out anything without a specific deadline and the spiritual self-care of your minister is often the first plate to hit the floor. The dangers inherent here are obvious. If your minister cannot stay fresh and renewed spiritually, both he and your congregation will suffer for it.

WHAT MIGHT HELP?

Things are not entirely hopeless. I don't believe the ministry is fated to be a career where those involved are destined to be run into the ground. If I thought that was the case there would be no reason for me to write this book. I am writing this book because I hope if enough church leaders read it, apply it, discuss it and address the issues we can salvage all of the great ministers who have yet to throw in the towel. In this specific matter I will offer you four suggestions. Two of them should be quite easy for you to implement. Two of them may be more challenging. We'll start with the easy and work our way up from there.

- ***Don't pile on plates***. *Discuss with* your minister what he is passionate about. What he is gifted for. Then as much as possible allow him to dedicate his time to those areas of ministry. *In consultation with* your minister remove tasks that can be done by someone other than him and then take it upon yourself – don't leave it to him – to find someone capable and competent to take on those tasks. Once your minister's desk has been streamlined, defend it. Don't allow other church members to dump new projects on your minister that don't require his particular involvement.
- ***Sabbath and Sabbaticals.*** We will discuss this at length in ***Reason #7***. In short, make sure your minister knows he is not expected to work an extreme amount of hours each week.

Encourage him to establish true days off (see **Reason #7** for definition). Make sure breaks and periods of rest and renewal are built in to his weekly, monthly and yearly schedules. Ensure that he has adequate time to be with and take care of the needs of his family and that he is doing so. I remember clearly when on one occasion I was asked how many hours I put in on an average week and one of my elders told me flat out "That's too much. You need to bring that number down." It was not easy to do, but it was completely liberating to know I had been authorized to bring my work hours down to a more suitable level – even if that meant some of the plates dropped.

- *Hire Executive Staff.* More and more churches are recognizing the need to free their minister up from many of the duties his position has accumulated. Some churches employ full or part time workers to handle much of the clerical and administrative tasks of their congregation. More recently, the churches that can afford to, have started hiring executive ministers to oversee the operational and organizational duties of the church. Having someone responsible for handling all of the business aspects of their church allows their other ministers to spend more time doing the ministry activities they got into ministry for in the first place.

- **Better train volunteers.** Part of the problem of trying to take things off of your minister's desk is that many of those things are important and still need to be done and done well. This brings us back to **Reason #1**. If the minister is not going to do those tasks any longer who is? If your church is not able to hire an executive minister, and many are not, then these duties must be assumed by volunteers. However some of these tasks are very important and can't be done by just anyone – that's why they ended up on the minister's desk in the first place. Whatever volunteer you recruit will need to be capable, competent and reliable. The tasks need to *get done, done well* and *done on time*. The reality is you may not have those kind of volunteers in your church at this moment. Therefore you will need to enact a very intentional plan to better develop and train your volunteers to take on and successfully complete some of these tasks.

REASON #6 (PART 1)
Trust-Busters

I cannot say for certain **Reason #6** is the biggest or the most common reason ministers choose to leave the ministry. I can say if you get **Reason #6** under control all the other reasons become a lot more manageable. Conversely, if you do not get **Reason #6** under control your odds of successfully working your way out of any of the other reasons are hugely diminished. **Reason #6** is all about relationships. A wide variety of relationships exist within a congregation and your minister must attempt to successfully navigate them all. Some of the things we have already looked at, (like volunteers, hijackers and critics) have a significant relational component to them. We won't cover that ground again, but instead we will focus our attention on what I believe are the key relational elements that can make or break your minister.

Without a doubt a minister's most important relationships in a church are his relationships with the church's leaders. Every church's leadership structure is a little bit different. Some churches have boards, others have elders and others have no designated leaders at all. There are two kinds of leaders in a church your minister needs to be aware. The first are those with the title and some degree of authority like an elder. The second are those who have no official title but are still unmistakably the opinion setters of the congregation. These can be a little harder to sniff out. It might be an elder or board member, or it might be a 75-year-old grandma, or a young couple that is extremely influential among all 25 – 45 year olds. Whoever they are, *both* the *opinion setters* and *decision makers* have to exist in harmony with your minister.

> SIDENOTE: Relational compatibility and complementary leadership styles between a candidate and existing church leaders may be one of the most important, and perhaps overlooked, factors when interviewing prospective ministers. If a church's minister and its leaders are not on the same page it is only a matter of time before critical problems arise.

As obvious as that might sound it is no easy thing. In fact it is a rather complex and bizarre thing. Relationships between a minister and the leaders of his church are somewhat of a paradox. On the one hand, the leaders are in authority over the minister. They hired him, they can fire him and they have the ability to veto his decisions. On the other hand, as members of the congregation these individuals are people the minister is trying to lead, equip, challenge and mature. It is also possibly that your minister has done more study and had more training in church leadership than some of your other church leaders. Clearly a conflict of interest exists and often presents challenges to the relationship between your minister and the other leaders of your church. Exactly how that is worked out may look slightly different in each unique congregation, but there is one thing I am absolutely positive is essential no matter what church you are in.

TRUST. Without trust between your leaders and your minister things are destined to deteriorate rapidly and end poorly. It is no coincidence it is going to take us three chapters to discuss the critical importance of a trusting relationship between church leaders and ministers. It has the potential to outweigh all the other *Reasons* combined – both in a good way and in a negative one. A trusting relationship does not come easy and it can be difficult to maintain at times, but the one thing you can be sure of is if trust is not established, maintained or re-created, someone will be walking out the door – it may be your minister, it may be your leaders, or it may be all of the above. Due to the nature of ministry and the tasks involved, it simply cannot be done outside of the context of trust. If trust does not exist, your minister may be able to keep the plates spinning for a while but his desire to do so will quickly evaporate. If trust does not exist your leaders will feel compelled to enact other parameters and requirements to fulfill the mandate of their responsibility as church leaders. Whatever measures are enacted are not put in place to frustrate the minister but rather because the leaders feel they have an obligation to the church as a whole to ensure the minister is accomplishing the goals the congregation called him to accomplish. Unfortunately the inevitable result of such requirements is almost always a further deterioration of the trust.

FOR MINISTERS ONLY:

Regardless of your experience, background or education you should not presume the existence of trust between you and your leaders when you first arrive at a new church. Trust must be built and built upon. One of your primary focuses in the initial weeks and months should be to spend as much time as possible developing those relationships of trust between you and the other leaders of your church. This is more important to your long-term health and effectiveness at your church than virtually anything else you could invest in at this point.

A trusting relationship between a minister and other church leaders can only be created gradually over time. Here is how it works: a small amount of trust is extended by the church leaders. Trust is graciously received and honored by the minister who reciprocates by extending a small amount of trust back to the church leaders. Back and forth it goes gradually building greater and greater levels of trust as individuals get to know each other better. Every time trust is rewarded by the faithful actions of one party or the other, new and greater trust is generated.

I am by no means a professional roofer, but I have nailed down my fair share of shingles over the years. The problem is I don't do it all the time and therefore when I do get up on the roof for the first time in a long time I'm not entirely comfortable. At first each step is very cautious and deliberate. My body is tense and my senses are on high alert for any indication I may be about to swan dive to the ground. With each step I take and do not fall off the roof confidence in my footing grows. With each passing minute my comfort level increases. Little by little. Step by step. That's exactly how trust is built in any relationship.

Of course the flip side of the coin is that every time trust is undermined by the actions of one party or another both sides drop back into a defensive posture. There are always those moments on the roof when I step on a patch where the asphalt pebble or the shingles are particularly loose. Without warning my feet begin to slide down toward the eaves. Panic sets in and my heart races. Usually the slide stops after only a few inches, but the longer the slide the more tentative my next moves become once it finally stops. Over time cautious steps begin to rebuild trust in my footing once again. Slowly but surely confidence grows and eventually I'm walking around in total comfort – doing cartwheels and backflips on the roof top! Okay, maybe not, but the point is, it takes constant and intentional effort to build trust in a relationship. It takes very little at all for things to snowball out of control and for trust to be completely obliterated. This deterioration of trust can be interrupted but only by a bold and risky leap of faith taken by one side or the other that extends a greater amount of trust regardless of events. This can be a frightening and extremely difficult thing to do regardless of which side you are on.

The relationship between a minister and his church leaders is in many ways similar to a marriage. The level of trust, communication, grace and cooperation required to make it work over the long haul is off the scales. There are some differences though. Most obviously, this is largely an arranged marriage. The courting period was likely only a few months where a handful of letters were exchanged, maybe a couple phone calls were made and one jam-packed weekend is the only face-to-face time spent together prior to the wedding. Not to mention your minister is marrying anywhere from two to twelve partners (church leaders) and inheriting dozens or hundreds of children (church members).

Not only is this relationship awkward by the sheer number of people involved, but it is complicated too. Your minister has to build, often from scratch, a connection with multiple church leaders, some of which he has very little in common with and whose personality is very different than his own. In addition, at any point for any reason his church leaders could serve him with divorce papers. It's not just that though, he also lives with the knowledge that any given week any one of his partners may decide they've had enough and resign or simply move away. Even more terrifying is that at some point - either at regular intervals or randomly depending on how your church appoints its leaders - a whole new crop of people could be added to the mix. Now he has to start all over and build his relationships with these new leaders. Worse yet, it is possible this new wave of leaders could shift the whole direction and mission of the congregation. Things he used to do with full authority are now questioned or unsupported. It is as though there is a new Pharaoh in Egypt who knew not Joseph and suddenly he's making bricks without straw. (cf. Exodus 1:8)

And then there's the kids. Church members who expect him to do everything the way the previous minister did. Others who expect him to do everything different than the previous minister did. Some who believe this is the perfect time to lobby him to back their agenda. Not to mention in all churches there is history between its members, some good – some ugly, which goes back sometimes for generations that he has no clue of. Church members will often talk with a church leader as a means to getting their minister to do or stop doing whatever it is that they think is best or heretical. Perhaps because they have a strong relationship with that particular leader or perhaps because they think they'll have a better chance of getting their way. One minister friend likened this situation to his kids coming to him to get him to persuade his wife to do something or to complain about all the things they didn't like or how their mom was so mean and unfair. He said, there is no way that would fly with me or my wife, but that's exactly what's happening with my leaders right now.

The process of building trust between a minister and the other leaders in your church is *simple though not easy*. Like building trust in any other relationship it takes determination and intentional effort. It requires assuming the best and granting the benefit of the doubt. It requires clear, regular and loving communication. More than anything it takes time and heaps of it. Not time in meetings and workshops, but time in living rooms and back yards, on boats and golf courses, at coffee shops and sporting events. Think about the people in your life who you feel like you can really trust. Then think about how much time you've spent with those people over the years. Now you're starting to get an idea of what we're talking about. It's a daunting task for church leaders to build this kind of relationship with their minister. Multiply that by the number of leaders your church has and you have a sense of what things feel like on your minister's side of the fence.

I am a regular at my local Starbucks. Over time I have come to know the baristas and they know me. I was chatting with one of them earlier this week. He called me by name which was a big step because for months he has been saying "Your name is ... Mark, right?" I told him not to feel bad because it is easy for me since they all wear name tags. He agreed and then added, "Plus you only have to learn half a dozen of us, we meet a whole bunch of people every day." Yeah, being a minister at a church is kinda like that.

SIDENOTE If you ever feel like your minister is a little aloof or you wish he would make more time to connect with you; if you wonder why he doesn't come over to your house more often or invite you over to his place more frequently; if you ever feel kind of put out that he didn't talk to you after worship service last Sunday - just bear in mind he's trying to build relationships with everyone in your church all at the same time. By virtue of sheer volume he simply can't give everyone the attention they – or he'd – like. He is regularly forced to prioritize where he invests his relationship building opportunities. His preference may be to sit and chat with you about the local sports team after church, but his role mandates that priority goes to meeting the new couple visiting for the first time this week, encouraging the single man who is struggling with his faith, connecting with the immigrant family who is still trying to find their place at your church or having a compassionate conversation with the lady who is trying to cope with the illness of a loved one. He wants to do these things too, he just doesn't have time to connect with everyone every week. And he may have

SIDENOTE (cont): loads of fun hanging out with your family in the park, but building his relationships with all of your church's current and future leaders has to take precedence. All that to say, sometimes he may actually prefer to be with you, but he needs to be with them. (And please don't take that to mean that if your minister talks to you right after service this Sunday that it is out of duty rather than desire).

Regardless of the difficulty, it is essential to the well-being of your minister, your leaders and your church. If you read the minister quotes at the beginning of this book you will have noticed that several highlighted the make it or break it power of a trust filled relationship between ministers and church leaders. I know far too many guys who have, sometimes after many years at a congregation, started sending out résumés because something had happened and whatever trust may have once existed was now gone and they were desperate to get out of that kind of relationship.

On the other hand the process of destroying trust between a minister and the other leaders in your church, is both *simple and easy*. There are likely countless ways for a minister to destroy his leaders trust in him. I will list a few of the most notorious ministerial trust-busters in the next chapter for the benefit of those readers who are currently serving in ministry. In the following chapter I will share with the rest of you some of the things that, from my experience and perspective, tend to erode a minister's trust in his leaders. Again, both these lists could probably be quite long, but I have chosen the culprits that in my opinion give you the most bang for your buck – but not in a good way.

REASON #6 (PART 2)
Leader's Trust-Busters

FOR MINISTERS ONLY:

Okay guys, I am no expert. I am not an elder or board member so I can't truly speak to this issue from their perspective. Thus far in my ministry career I have not been a chronic destroyer of my church leader's trust – at least as far as I know – and on occasions when I have done so I have been blessed with church leaders who were gracious enough to look over it and get past it. Therefore most of what I'm about to share with you is from observation and from talking with some of the church leaders I know.

By the way, if you are a church leader who just totally ignored my *"For Minister's Only"* heading, way to go! You just destroyed all the trust, man! Just kidding. It's no biggie and I forgive you. However, since you're reading this anyway, let me say this: The number one thing on your list in the next chapter is [SPOILER ALERT] "Poor Communication" so if you read the remainder of this chapter and say to yourself, "He's got it all wrong. Those things definitely destroy trust, but there's a whole lot of things that are a whole lot worse." Then would you please, please, please kindly let your minister know what those things are because I obviously don't have a clue and he needs to know. Much obliged.

Poor Communication

Not surprisingly, this tops my list of trust-busters in both this chapter and the next. However the way it manifests is different on both sides of the pulpit. Here's what I've observed: most church leaders, even the good ones who are not micromanagers, like to know what's going on. One of the most unpleasant things that can happen to your church leaders is for someone in your congregation to ask them a question about something you are doing and for them to have to reply "I know nothing about that." Such a scenario often leaves them feeling as though they are not adequately performing the functions of their office. After all, how can they possibly be leading the church if they don't even know what the minister is doing? Of course most church leaders, especially the very good ones, have no desire to be micromanagers. They know for them to monitor the minutia of your work is not only a hassle for you, but it is a horribly inefficient use of their time as well. And there's the rub. How can leaders stay apprised of what you're doing without wasting a whole lot of your time *and* their time needlessly? Good communication can help.

Therefore, as much as possible keep your leaders informed about what you are doing. Tell them about the things you are working on, what things are going well and what things that you are having issues with.

Keep them up-to-date. Give them the picture in the broad strokes but be prepared to fill in the details should they ask for further clarification.

Do not make assumptions about what your leaders think or want. I have known ministers who assumed that no response from their church leaders meant consent or approval. I have also known ministers who assumed no response from their church leaders meant "no." I have seen them both be wrong. Here is what I've come to understand: no response from your church leaders means ... wait for it ... nothing. It doesn't mean yes. It doesn't mean no. It only means they haven't answered. If you have not got an answer from your leaders on a particular issue do not move forward until you do. If you absolutely need a response then communicate with them clearly and state "Unless I hear from you otherwise by this specific date I will move ahead with this plan."

If your church leaders start to feel like you are leaving them out of the loop or doing things without keeping them informed the natural human inclination is to start to wonder if there is a reason you're not telling them everything. Are you doing something you don't want them to know about? Are you not doing something you don't want them to find out about? If these kinds of questions hover around long enough, church leaders begin to feel the need to check into things themselves to find out what's really going on. This is easily mistaken by ministers as a lack of trust and so the downward spiral begins.

Insubordination

Insubordination might be too strong of a word, but it is the one that seemed to fit best. They say if you are ever attacked by a bear what you should do is make yourself look as big as possible. Hopefully the bear will be intimidated, back down and run away. This tends to be the human response to most things. Whenever we feel threatened we try and make ourselves look big and powerful. When a minister becomes defiant or disregards the instructions of his church leaders the end result is never good. Odds are, if you attack your leaders they are going to respond by doing something to make themselves look big and powerful to remind you who is in charge.

SIDENOTE: Although there are some church leaders who are power hungry control freaks (there are also some ministers who are equally so), my experience has been that most church leader respond this way motivated not by the lust for power or due to a slighted ego, but rather they see it as their God-given, church-appointed duty to be responsible for what happens in your congregation – including what you do.

If you want your church leaders to be there for you, stand behind you and back you up then you have to be willing to submit to their direction. As I mentioned earlier in this chapter the relationship between the minister and his church leaders is a bizarre one. As minister, you are simultaneously trying to lead your leaders and submit to their leadership. It is not always easy to know how best to do that. Sometimes ministers attempted to push ahead with what they think is best because they can't get a clear answer from their leaders. Sometimes ministers push ahead out of frustration. Sometimes it is less an open defiance than it is board room bullying.

I am a thinker. I often feel like Hannibal Smith in the A-Team movie who says, "Give me an hour and I'm good. Give me a week and I'm even better. Give me six months and I'm unbeatable." When there is an issue at hand I think about it and think about it and think about it. I think that thing to death. I figure out all the angles, I analyze all the data and then I craft the perfect argument in my mind. I select all the right words. I anticipate all the counter arguments. And then I rehearse my argument in my mind until I know it so well I could say it in a coma. I recall a time several years ago when my elders and I were having an ongoing discussion about completing time charts. When you read the next chapter you'll find out exactly how I feel about time charts. I remember vividly one meeting we had and I came in loaded for bear. I was going to put an end to this discussion once and for all and I had the perfect argument to do it. So when the time came I laid it all out there with great eloquence. Let's not forget I talk for a living. I wasn't rude or mean, I spoke calmly and politely. I asked them all the right questions that would get me all the right answers. I verbally walked them down the path I wanted them to go and when I had them lined up perfectly on the bull's-eye I lowered the proverbial boom of my rationale. My argument was flawless, my logic was sound. And I walked out of that meeting having won the battle, and totally lost the war. I may have made what I considered to be advances on the time chart issue, but I had undeniably lost some of their trust – and rightfully so. It would take some time for my leaders and I to rebuild the trust obliterated by that and several other events around that time.

Bottom line: If you want your leaders to be willing to take a bullet for you – you can't be the one holding the gun.

Always Asking

Let me start this section by giving your leadership the benefit of the doubt: I choose to believe that most church leaders want to do what is best for their minister and for their church. I choose to believe that most church leaders want to help, assist and support their minister in any way they can. I know there are exceptions but for now we will assume that this is the norm. My experience with church leaders has generally been that as long as they feel like the trust they have extended has been rewarded with faithful service they are relatively open to requests expressed by the minister. But there is a delicate balance here that must be maintained. If your grocery list exceeds your recent performance your church leaders will more than likely become less liberal in granting your requests.

This delicate balance kind of reminds me of playing Jenga. When you are playing Jenga things usually go relatively well as long as the pace at which you are removing blocks from the bottom keeps in step with the pace you are adding blocks to the top. When done right the tower can actually be relatively tall. Unless you're playing with that guy Larry who always insists on taking the middle piece out of every level. However if, instead of taking one brick out of the bottom and putting one brick on the top, you started to take five bricks out of the bottom and put one brick on the top, your tower would not get built nearly as high and it would become unstable and crash much quicker. Even more so if you took 10 bricks out of the bottom and put one on top.

In the minister/church leader relationship there is a balance of give-and-take, or more appropriately a balance of give-and-give. As long as your church leaders feel like you are putting in to your ministry in proportion to what you are asking to get from them, you will most likely be able to work together harmoniously. But if your requests come too great or too fast or your personal investment in your ministry significantly diminishes it will give your leaders pause – and rightfully so. After all, they are charged with being good stewards of the churches resources which includes both the finances *and the staff*.

I experienced this to a small degree in my first church over what turned out to be a clerical error. The problem was, being new and fresh out of school and not knowing any better I made an error in keeping track of my days worked. Specifically the error was in regard to vacation time. Whenever I went on vacation for a week I blocked off seven days. However, what I should have done was block off five days of vacation time and two days off. Because of this glitch when I handed in my record of days worked at the end of the year it appeared to my church leaders that instead of taking my allotted 15 days of vacation time, I had taken 21 days. Unfortunately, neither of us really noticed this error until my final year at that church. When I knew I would be moving away I purposefully saved two weeks of vacation to give us time to make the move, or better yet be paid out to help with the relocation expenses. However, because according to the records it seemed as though I had been taking an extra week of vacation time each of the four years I had been working there, in the end I did not get paid out for those two weeks I thought I had remaining. Of course, from their perspective I was still walking away with two extra weeks.

I've watched ministers at other churches ask and ask and ask. "Can I have this? Can I do that? Can you give me more? Can I do less?" And I have watched as normally generous leaders have gradually become fed up and eventually said "No more." Not because the requests were so extreme or unreasonable (at least not most of them) but simply because the balance between what the church was putting into the minister and what the church was getting out of the minister grew to be wildly disproportionate from the church leaders perspective.

SIDENOTE: I'm not saying you should never ask for anything. You will recall at the start of this book I encouraged you to be your own advocate and speak up when you need something or are struggling. That advice still holds, just be conscious and aware of the pace at which those requests come and make sure that your leaders are feeling confident about the work you are putting in before soliciting them for something new.

Colleagues

I won't say much on this point except to say this: you need to be aware if you are at a multi-staff church your church leaders, at least to a degree, will view all the staff as one entity. Therefore, if your church leaders are having significant issues of trust with one of the other ministers on your staff, some of that tension will inevitably and unavoidably spill over onto you. There is nothing you can do except stay out of it as much as you can and make extra efforts to show your church leaders they can trust you.

A similar dynamic can exist when your leaders have had trust issues with a former minister you have replaced. Of course, the danger is you will take it personally and will reciprocate this vicarious lack of trust by withdrawing some of your trust from your church leaders. In return your church leaders who are already on heightened alert because of the issues they are having with your colleague will react to your removal of trust and the whole thing can spin out of control rapidly.

WHAT MIGHT HELP?

Numerous things can be done to prevent the loss of trust between you and your church leaders. Here are a couple of the most effective:

- **Build in advance.** One of the best things you can do is build a relationship with your church leaders long before the problem arises. The greater trust you have built with your church leaders in advance, the easier it will be to weather and recover from any issues you may have down the road. Do not wait until a crisis of trust exists to try and build your relationship with your church leaders. Think of it as if you were driving down the highway and you knew you were about to pass the last gas station you would see in a long time. If you were smart you would pull off and top up your tank just to make sure you had enough fuel to get where you were going. What you don't want to do is end up out of gas in the middle of nowhere. When the gauge hits "E" it's too late to look for a fuel station. Likewise, fill up your trust tank in advance, before you need it, and if possible fill a jerry can or two also.

- **_Ask them_**. This seems painfully obvious, but I will throw it out there anyways. Talk to your church leaders. Ask them what kind of things shake their trust in you. When you start to sense that something is a little wonky ask them about. "Did something happen? Is something wrong? Did I do something you are upset with?" One little question can save you a whole lot of misery. Even if the question, and more so the answer, is uncomfortable for you it is infinitely better than the alternative. You don't have to be paranoid about every little look they give you or thing they say, but stay on top of it and don't be afraid to be the first one to address the issue.

- ***Make the leap***. There are two ways to correct your leaders' diminished trust. The first is to put extra effort into making yourself unquestionably trustworthy. The second is to fight your natural instinct to take a defensive posture and instead go out on a limb and extend to your leaders a larger portion of your trust. Granted it is a little risky and it is possible you may get burned by it, but someone has to break the cycle and, if you really want things to change, it might as well be you.

REASON #6 (PART 3)
Minister's Trust-Busters

Now we flip to the other side of the coin. The previous chapter looked at the ways a minister can diminish the trust his church leaders have in him. In this chapter, we will examine some of the things, in my opinion, church leaders do – often inadvertently – can significantly diminish the minister's trust in them. Trust is a two-way street and without *both* ministers *and* church leaders working together intentionally and relentlessly to build that relationship of trust, our churches will be plagued by conflict. Here are my top three trust-busters for church leaders.

Poor Communication

Nothing destroys trust in *any* relationship more than poor communication. George Bernard Shaw is quoted as saying, "The single biggest problem with communication is the illusion that it has taken place." When communication is poor between your leaders and your minister, your minister is forced to assume which causes all sorts of problems. If your minister assumes incorrectly, he can get himself in trouble by inadvertently going against the leaders wishes. This always seems to backfire in one of two ways. In some cases the leaders will lose trust in the minister because he has done something they feel they did not authorize him to do. In other cases the leaders will confront the minister about what he has done. At this point he will feel betrayed, as though the rug had been pulled out from underneath his feet. He believed he had received the leaders support and now it has been rescinded. This typically leaves the minister feeling like he has been hung out to dry, embarrassed or reprimanded. Obviously, and understandably, this deteriorates the minister's trust in the leaders.

There are several different factors that can contribute to poor communication. Some of the most common causes are:

- Statements are unclear or messages are mixed
- When feedback and opinions are not shared
- When individual thoughts and perspectives are voiced but no group decision is ever reached
- When not enough information is shared or decisions are not thoroughly explained
- Not listening closely enough or not remembering previous discussions

Your minister and your church leaders quite likely have different backgrounds, different experiences, different perspectives and different personalities. They also have different ways of sharing ideas, expressing themselves and viewing the world. This is further amplified when your minister and leaders come from different generations. In these situations it is not only possible, but likely, the two parties can say the exact same thing but understand completely different messages.

I recall one occasion when a co-worker of mine met with the leaders of our church to discuss a certain matter. Within a few days of that meeting, I talked to one of our elders and got his assessment of the discussions and conclusions that came out of the meeting. A few days later, I had an opportunity to talk with my co-worker. He also described to me the discussions and conclusions from the meeting. I am not exaggerating one tiny, little bit when I say I would have sworn that those two men were in two completely different meetings. I cannot see any possible way those two reports came from the same discussion. I kid you not, they literally told me the exact opposite thing. The good news was they were both quite happy with how the meeting had turned out. The bad news was it was not long before miscommunication took its toll.

Tracking Time

Let me begin by stating this: when I was in my late teens and early 20s and interned with churches during the summer break, I was required to complete time charts. That made sense to me because I was an intern and was at times helpful as I learned to develop some time management skills. We currently have an intern at our church under my supervision and I make him fill out time charts. They're much less detailed than the ones I had to complete but they still serve a purpose.

I also occasionally do time charts for my own benefit and I know other ministers who do the same. When I do chart my time I do it only for a season and I do it meticulously. By meticulously I mean my charts cover 24 hours each day and are broken down into one minute intervals. For me this is essential because my day, particularly at work, does not break up into one hour or half hour blocks – it is made up of 7 minutes, 12 minutes, 3 minutes, 10 minutes, 18 minutes, 2 minute activities. The reason I occasionally chart my time is to help me clarify how my time is being used, where my time is going, and if there are any changes I need to make. My criteria for change is simply this: I want to be spending most of my time in the areas I feel I am most gifted and the areas that are most important to my ministry.

Generally speaking, I have a fairly good intuitive sense of where my time is going and how much time is being spent on this or that. Nonetheless the occasional season of charting helps affirm that my gut feeling is still accurate and allows me to make recalibrations when needed. I don't always chart my time, but when I do, I chart *all* my time. I not only keep track of my time at work, but I keep track of my time outside of work as well. I track the time I spend with my wife and with my kids, the time I spend on leisure activities, the time I spend watching TV and movies, the time I spend on household chores, even the time I spend on things like showering and eating. I chart *everything*. The reason I do this is because I'm not only interested in how much time I spend at work each week but I also want to know if the rest of my life is in balance. I don't just care how long it takes me to prepare a sermon each week, I care if my family is getting the time it needs and how many hours I'm frittering away on Facebook.

When I chart my time I usually do it for at least two or three months. I do this because my life and particularly my work are rarely the same from week to week. Let me explain:

- I can go months without making a visit to the hospital and then have three people to visit in one week.
- I preach at our congregation almost every week, but as luck would have it I spoke a couple days ago and now I don't speak once in the next four Sundays.
- Weddings happen in the summer which means pre-marriage counseling happens in the spring.
- In the summer I spend extra time planning sermon series for the upcoming year and small group activities for the fall.
- Special services like Christmas and Easter come only a few times a year. Other projects also come along randomly and periodically.

Charting for one week or even one month would not give a remotely balanced or accurate assessment of my time usage. I'm not saying that this is what everyone should do, it's just what works for me.

That being said, one of the most damaging things church leaders can do to the trust of their minister is *require* him to complete and *hand in* time charts. I will concede that sometimes, with some ministers, leaders may feel that time charts are necessary, but they come with a price. There is an inherent flaw with the idea of having a minister chart his work time. The problem is that a minister's time cannot be clearly or easily charted. So much of what a minister does with his time is nebulous and fluid. It becomes extremely difficult to accurately reflect in simple blocks of time. Requiring a minister to complete and hand in time charts on a regular and consistent basis has numerous drawbacks. Here are some of the most dangerous:

- *They don't work*. Time charts simply do not convey the information church leaders really want to know. Either the charts are too general which really tells church leaders nothing, or the charts are so detailed and specific that church leaders are faced with more raw data than they are able or interested in processing.
- *They are tedious*. As I mentioned above when I do time charts I meticulously break them down into one minute intervals. I do this because I believe it is necessary to get a truly accurate representation of where and how much time is being used. The problem is, it is horrifically tedious. It is a constant hassle and

a regular distraction. Even a time chart broken down into slightly larger intervals would still be an ongoing annoyance for your minister to complete.

- **_They force your minister to categorize_**. As soon as you ask your minister to complete and turn in a timesheet, he knows you will be looking at how many hours he has logged and reviewing whether or not that amount of hours is sufficient. This forces your minister to assess and categorize every activity he is involved in based on the criteria of: is it work or is it not work. The challenge here is twofold:
  1. It is extremely difficult. Many activities are rather ambiguous to a minister. During these moments it is virtually impossible to determine whether time should be classified as work time or not work time. For example, if I come over to your house for dinner one evening is it work time or is it not work time? Well, it depends. If I am there because you are a future leader and I am trying to mentor you or because you seem discouraged and I'm trying to encourage you, then perhaps it's work time. If I'm there because all the members of our church are encouraged to visit with other members and build those relationships then perhaps it is work time or perhaps it is not. If I am there because I enjoy hanging out with you

and we share a common love of Star Wars – the original three not the prequels obviously – then perhaps it is not work time. But what if it is all of the above or two out of three then how should it be classified?

And what about worship times or small group times or general fellowship times? Sure, these are things we want all of the members of our church to do. On the other hand regular members are not *required* to be there like someone on staff would be. Then again lots of people in the congregation take leadership roles in these activities so that is in some ways the same. On the other, other hand it is not exactly the same because I'm not a volunteer and I don't get the choice. I am the minister and I cannot take off my minister's hat. It's nebulous, murky, unclear.

2. But perhaps even worse than being difficult, it takes the joy out of ministry. You see, I can no longer just come over to your house and call it ministry. I have to call it work or not work. I end up feeling obliged to squeeze in another appointment just to get my hours fulfilled that week. Or I feel inclined to turn down invitations and requests

because I've already maxed out my hours for the week.

By its very nature, requiring time charts from your minister creates a combative relationship between church leaders and ministers. The problems time charts create are:

1. They initially send the message that the leaders are not confident that the minister is using his time appropriately or that he is able to manage his own time effectively.
2. They create paranoia in the minister over who will be skimming through their charts and independently assessing all of their activities.

Both of these things are nuclear bombs to trust.

Waffling

Mmm, waffles. In this case however, waffles are not a good thing. One of the most important things from a minister's point of view is to know where your leaders stand and to be confident they will be there when he needs them. Sometimes this is tied to poor communication as mentioned above. It's not so much that leaders have flip-flopped on their position, but it is the by-product of poor communication the minister misunderstood their position initially so now it appears as though the leaders' position has changed. At other times a minister may get a clear indication from his leaders, however when reaction and resistance comes from certain segments of the congregation, the leaders may reverse their position which obviously leaves the minister in an extremely vulnerable place.

It is critical to the trust the minister has in his leaders that he is confident the leaders will be there to back him up and support him. We've already discussed the impact hijackers and critics can have on your minister. This impact can be minimized if your church has strong leaders who are willing to stand behind your minister. On the other hand, this impact will be magnified if you don't – or if your leaders are among those creating the problem. When church leadership waffles on its position or neglects to stand behind its minister it does not take very long for the minister to lose confidence in them. He quickly learns he cannot count on them to be there when the bullets start flying.

Most ministers will respond to this revelation in one of two ways.

1. **Go to ground**. Having realized he is on his own, some ministers will take the "duck and cover" approach. Don't stir anything up. Don't rock the boat. Avoid ruffling feathers. This inhibits your minister's ability to challenge your church to grow and mature. It also, very likely, diminishes his joy and enthusiasm for the work he is doing.

2. **Go rogue**. Some ministers will go the exact opposite direction. Instead of just going with the flow they will purposefully go against it. They will stop seeking the leaders input,

opinions or endorsement because they know the odds are high that the leaders may change their minds anyway. Ministers in this situation can easily become aggressive and resentful.

I recall hearing a story from a minister who once played a video in his church, something that had been deemed completely acceptable, even desirable, by his elders. However on this occasion, a small number of people in the congregation objected – not to the content of the video itself, but simply to the use of any video during worship. In response to these comments the elders retracted their previous endorsement of playing videos, leaving the minister feeling very much like the scapegoat. Not only did he feel like he had been reprimanded for doing something that had been fully authorized, but he also felt as though the critics had been given a trump card by his own leaders.

WHAT MIGHT HELP?

Thankfully, on this count, there are plenty of things that I think can be done and most of them are not incredibly difficult. Here are just a few of the things I believe will help build trust in the relationship between your church's minister and its leaders:

- ***Spend time together***. Part of building a relationship of trust is simply building a relationship. The more your minister and church leaders can spend time together outside of church service and elder/board meetings the more friendship and trust can be built between them. I am a strong proponent of ministers and church leaders spending time together socially, not just when discussing church business, but purely having fun together.

- **Inclusion**. Nothing creates suspicion, uneasiness, defensiveness or lack of trust quicker than excluding someone from a discussion or decision. If you want to eliminate poor communication a great place to start is to make sure everyone who is involved in a situation is in the room when it is being discussed – that way everyone knows what was said and decided because they were there.

SIDENOTE Whenever your minister and church leaders have a discussion together make sure somebody takes notes. If it all possible have two people take notes because it is so easy for one person to miss something - especially if people keep talking while they are trying to write the notes. If the discussion is held outside a regular meeting, designate someone to write down the general discussion and decision of the group and give copies to everyone else to verify everyone heard and agreed upon the same thing. Always have a written or electronic copy of decisions so you can go back at a later date and confirm what has been agreed upon.

- **Have regular personal dialogue**. What I've found works better than requiring time charts is for ministers and church leaders to have regular personal visits with one another. Leaders can walk away from these meetings with a much better sense of what the minister is doing, his struggles and his needs, his goals and how they can help. Ministers can leave these meetings feeling like they have been heard, understood and supported. I would recommend your minister sit down with a church leader – not necessarily always the same one – over a nice cup of coffee every two or three months. This is *not* a performance review it is a "How are things going?" conversation.

- ***Be clear and consistent***. One of the greatest gifts your church leaders can give your ministers is the confidence to know that no matter what happens they have his back. A minister will be able to survive and overcome a lot of other challenges if he knows that his church leaders trust him and that he can trust them. As a church leader be sure to regularly tell your minister "We are completely behind you." It is equally important to make it clear to the other members of your congregation that, as a leadership, you are fully behind your minister as well.

SIDENOTE If there is one thing I have learned in the process of authoring this book it is this: It is really easy to write things wrong. To write in a way that is clear, easily understood and not easily misread is usually difficult, sometimes impossible. Written communication lacks tone, inflection and body language and therefore can be easily misinterpreted and misunderstood. Email can be a useful tool for sharing benign information, but face to face is by far the best media for discussion.

REASON #7 (PART 1)
Stressors

Here we are at last, **Reason #7**! In this chapter we are going to talk about stress. It could be argued that the previous **6 Reasons** all create stress and that's a fair assessment. However the items in this chapter are more about helping your minister deal with the stress all that other stuff can cause. These things can minimize the impact of the other stresses of ministry if they are handled well. On the other hand, if handled poorly, these things will amplify everything else that frustrates your minister and hasten his departure from your church or ministry altogether. Because I'm a sucker for alliteration, I've labelled these stresses: salaries, supplementals, support, sabbaths and sabbaticals. I imagine for many of you when you picked up this book and read its title these are some of the first things that came to your mind. Perhaps you've been expecting this chapter, turning each page cautiously waiting for the hammer to fall. Perhaps some of you are thinking to yourselves, "I knew it! I knew that one way or another this was all going to come back to wanting more money, more benefits, or time off." However, I want you to know that I have not hidden these things in the last chapter simply to string you along. They're not in **Reason #7** because I think they are the most important or the most urgent items to be addressed

– they are not the climax of this book. The truth is, I do think *all* of these things are *extremely important* and yet they are all things that historically the church has been extremely negligent in providing for its ministers. I think that should change. Nonetheless, I'm also convinced that you could totally nail **Reason #7**, I mean completely knock it out of the park, but if you don't address **Reasons #1-6** the odds of keeping your minister are still slim to none.

I am a card-carrying member of S.E.S.P.U. – that stands for South East Saskatchewan Preachers Union. Of course it's not a *real* union. I will tell you more about what we really do a little later. The truth is ministers have no union. In a denomination like mine where every congregation is autonomous we don't even have an overseeing board that ensures the minister at one church receives the same salary and benefits as the minister at another church. My guess is that most people in most churches don't have a clue what the minister receives in terms of salary and benefits let alone what the minister down the road receives. In some ways I actually like that. I have to tell you, there is nothing more awkward for a minister than sitting in the Annual General Meeting every year with his salary displayed on the screen as the congregation discusses their yearly budget. How many of you would allow me to print your salary in next week's bulletin (let alone permit the congregation to vote on whether your income should be increased or decreased)? Yeah, I didn't think so. So on the one hand, I don't mind the anonymity.

On the other hand, sometimes a little enlightenment might be useful. I recall a conversation several years ago following an AGM when one of our members came up to me and said, "I can't believe that's what you get paid. How do you live on that? And you don't even have any benefits." I'll admit my heart was warmed by his empathetic assessment. I'll also admit I wish he would have spoken up in the meeting and said, "Hey folks, this is ridiculous! Surely there's a way we can do something better." But he didn't. No one did.

In retrospect, I have no huge grievances over the financial compensation I have received over the years. Not every minister can say that – at least not with a straight face. I don't know if your church is adequately caring for your minister in regard to salary and benefits. I truly hope you are and if you are not I hope reading this chapter will inspire you to work towards that goal. So please don't take this as whining or complaining. This is neither an accusation nor an ultimatum. I simply want to share with you some of the things I feel would be appropriate for churches to provide for ministers – even if I wasn't one. If you agree great! If you disagree, that's fine, as long as you can explain for yourself why.

My eight year old son loves Lego. Last spring, for his birthday he told us he didn't want a party or a bunch of presents, all he wanted was to go to Lego Kidsfest in a nearby city. As it turned out we were able to make that work. I vividly remember one session where my son was sitting in the middle of the room with the rest of the hundred kids who lined up early enough to get in. I was sitting by the wall with the all the other parents. The kids sat mesmerized as they listened to a Lego Masterbuilder describe all the things that Lego can do. Then he asked the question, "How many of you kids have seen the Lego Movie?" Ninety-nine arms shot up into the air so fast and so high they almost dislocated themselves from their shoulder sockets. One little boy in the front row looked around and then looked at me with big puppy dog eyes. We had really wanted to see the movie, but it just didn't work out for us to get to the theater so we were anxiously waiting on the DVD release. All I wanted to do was run out there and give him a big hug and say, "I'm really sorry, buddy." However, I chose to spare him the embarrassment and just gave a reassuring smile instead.

Every minister I have talked to about this issue has told me the same thing: "It's not that I'm greedy, I just feel like I'm disappointing my family and that, more than anything, makes me want to pick up the want ads." I image your minister is likely the same. If it were just him he could suck it up, make do and get by. He could accept the fact he'll never have a cabin at the lake or travel to New York. The truth is, part of him likely feels guilty for even desiring those things in the first place.

But it's not just him. He has a daughter who has friends – even church friends – who go to Disneyland every year, but she's never been once. He has a son who wants to join the hockey team with his buddies, but the equipment and registration fees are too costly. He has a wife with a sister who went to Hawaii for her anniversary, but your minister and his wife spent their last anniversary in Montana's – the restaurant, not the state.

Family vacations are not planned based on what exotic location they'd like to visit next, but how much gas they can put in the car – assuming it makes it there and back again – and who they know along the way and at their destination so they can stay for free. I've heard ministers lament they were unable to send their wife home for the wedding or funeral of a close family member because they had no means to purchase the plane ticket.

I recall conversations in our own house where the question was asked, "I need new shirts, you need new pants, and the kids need new shoes: which one can we afford to get?" Sometimes the answer was "None of the above." The kids don't often complain, his wife rarely says anything, but he knows deep down they feel it, and he knows that it is all because *he* made the choice to be in ministry and it weighs on him like a sack of rice in a rainstorm.

FOR MINISTERS ONLY:
If you're in ministry, odds are your income is limited. I hope that changes for you someday soon, but in the meantime: you can't live like a king when you're getting paid like a pauper. One of the worst things you can do to yourself and your family is to live beyond your means and rack up debt (regardless of how fair or unfair you think your wage is). Debt is easy to accumulate and tough to get rid of. Do yourself a favor and find whatever way possible to not live on borrowed money.

Your minister is not a selfish, greedy, money grabbing malcontent. However the reality is, your minister might stick with your church when times get tough and the hours get long; he may endure the critics and put up with the hijackers; he may work through problems, live in a fishbowl and put the effort into building trust with your leaders; he might hang in there and do all these things *if* his salary and benefits package allows him to more than adequately take care of his family. However, if paying the bills and providing for his family is just one more added stress being in ministry brings, then you can't blame him for looking for another better paying profession *without* all those other hassles. Lots of people will stick with a bad job if it comes with good pay. No one sticks with a bad job with bad pay any longer than they absolutely have to.

Salaries

Minister's salaries have always been a complicated thing. I remember my dad telling me that when he first started working for the church they held a men's business meeting – that's how things were done back then – to decide how much he should get paid. Everyone wrote a figure on a piece of paper and handed it in. One person wrote $200 per month. This was in the early 70s, but it was still a ridiculously low amount.

The man reasoned the minister should not get paid more than the lowest paid person in the congregation and since he was currently getting $200 per month on welfare he figured that's how much my dad should be making also. In the end the group decided to pay him slightly more than that amount, however, he had to go on the road and visit other churches in an attempt to raise the money himself. I've heard of ministers being paid based on the average income of the entire congregation. I know other ministers who lived through the era where their salary was determined by the number of children they had. The only time they got a raise was when a new kid was born. My wife is unspeakable thankful times have changed.

Even now deciding how much your minister should get paid is a challenge. Part of the problem is there is no universal standard. You cannot go on the Internet and look up the pay grid for ministers like you can for a teacher. The statistics that you can find vary greatly depending on where you live, education, years of experience and what denomination you belong to.

Ministry is a unique job. There really aren't any good parallels.

So how should your church decide how much your minister gets paid? I don't know. What I do know is that you should pay him enough that he can adequately care for his family and live comfortably in your community. I suggest you do your homework. Call around to other churches in your denomination or churches that are in your city but outside your denomination and see how much they are paying their minister and what their pay scale is based on.

Personally, I think one of the best places to start is to ask yourself, "How much would I want the wage to be if this was my job?" I remember the years when we had both our boys in daycare. I recall thinking childcare was ridiculously expensive every time I had to write out the monthly cheque. Then one day I did the math. I divided the cost per child per day by the number of hours my kids attended the daycare. I immediately thought, "There's no way I would watch someone else's kid all day for such a meager amount." Of course, there is more than one child at daycare so the caregiver's wage is multiplied by the number of kids but then again, so is the work required. And the mess and the noise. And I thought, "There is NO WAY I would do all that for that wage."

Perhaps another good approach would be to ask, "How comfortable would my life be if my salary were adjusted to this level?" Just for fun try to rework your personal budget as if you were living on your minister's take home paycheck.

More than anything I would like to see churches set the standard for being generous in what they pay their staff – and not just because I want a raise. I genuinely believe that the way the church cares for its employees should be a strong witness to the world about who we are trying to be. A minister's job is stressful enough as it is. You are doing yourself a huge favor to remove any financial stress from an inadequate salary from the equation.

SIDENOTE I know in the past some have viewed a minister's reduced salary as just part of their sacrifice for the LORD and postulated the minister will be rewarded for that by God. However I tend to think it would be even better if churches paid their ministers an appropriate salary and allowed them to be examples of godly stewardship and sacrificial giving out of those funds. It is a challenge for some ministers to do those things when they are living on a shoestring budget to begin with. It also can create an extremely awkward

SIDENOTE (cont): situation when your minister is
called to challenge people in your church to greater
giving and better stewardship of their own money.
Not to mention, most ministers I know take their
salary - whatever it may be - and return a portion
of it into the collection plate each Sunday, which
in some ways is like paying a portion of your own
pay cheque.

Supplementals

In addition to salary, there are several other benefits
that would be worthwhile for you to offer to your
minister. The absence of these benefits affects how
far your minister's salary can go, and how generous
he can be with others. Here are some things to
consider adding to your minister's benefit package.

- Pension/RRSPs: Whether the church
  contributes on its own accord or does so on a
  matching basis with the minister, in today's
  world providing some kind of pension option is
  an absolute must. I have seen too many
  ministers not have the means to retire when
  the time comes. Long after their peers have
  started spending winters in Hawaii and
  summers traveling the country to visit
  children and grandchildren, ministers
  continue to work in churches and Walmarts
  and donut shops simply to sustain themselves
  through their twilight years. Whether it is
  because no benefits are provided or because
  they receive such a limited salary they are not

able to put money into their own pension plan this certainly needs to be corrected.

- Extended Health Care: Naturally this depends on where you live and what standard healthcare is available to your minister. Nonetheless whether strictly by church contribution or on a matching basis you should ensure that your minister is able to provide for the health care needs of his family including items like dentistry, eye care, disability and life insurance. I have known ministers who would have liked to stay in ministry but simply could not afford to. When their kids needed braces or their wife needed expensive medications these ministers were forced out of the pulpit to seek out jobs that would provide increased income and/or adequate additional insurance.

- Professional Development: It is in your church's best interest to provide adequate funds *and* time allotments for your minister to be involved in professional development and ongoing education activities. Your minister needs these times of continued learning, new inspiration and fresh ideas. Workshops, seminars and classes are not cheap, especially if you factor in the costs of travel, food and accommodations. It is not fair to make your minister have to choose between a vacation with his family or attending a workshop and seminar. Without allotted time *and* sufficient funds for these activities this is the choice most ministers face.

- <u>Mission Leave</u>: I believe it is incredibly valuable to your minister and your church to have both time and funds designated to allow him to become involved in short term foreign missions. Not only will this refresh and invigorate him which will translate into new enthusiasm and vision for your church's mission at home, but he will quite often take others from your congregation along on the mission trip which will impact them greatly and instill in them a much broader sense of the Kingdom and a heart for missions for years to follow. Over time this can have a dramatic impact on your congregation as a whole.

- Benevolence Leave: Allot time and perhaps even a travel stipend for your minister to take his family to memorial services for his or his wife's immediate family members (parents, siblings or grandparents). These are truly important life moments and it would be a shame for your minister – who is asked to console your congregation members in their loss – to not have opportunity to grieve with his family in these times. This issue will not come up often, but when it does your minister will feel tremendously blessed by such a provision.

- Marriage Investment: I know this one is a little more out there, but consider what benefit there might be to your congregation for you to arrange for your minister and their spouse to have a weekend away once every six or twelve months. Your minister is only as strong and stable as his marriage and his spouse are. When spouses, regardless of their profession, do not invest enough time in one another marriages breakdown. Your minster is not immune to this reality. Many ministers would say they rarely have time for a date night with their spouse let alone take a whole weekend away. And even if they could swing the time, the reality is a minister's salary often doesn't allow the means for such a *frivolous* excursion. I will never forget the time a young couple in our church gave my wife and I a weekend at the bed-and-breakfast on the Sunshine Coast just to let us know they appreciated us and the work we were doing. It was a wonderful weekend and an incredible encouragement to us. It was also, without a doubt, something we would have never been able to do on our own dime.

- <u>Other Expenses</u>: At some churches the minister is required to buy books to study from, a computer to work on, regular cups of coffee and lunches as he meets with his congregants and pay for parking every time he visits someone in the hospital – one of the most expensive places to park in my experience. Some of these things are quite costly, others aren't so bad the first time, but quickly start to add up. Consider ways to reimburse your minister for these work expenses or find creative ways of compensating him for these out of pocket purchases.

- <u>More Creative Ideas</u>: Even the small things can have an impact. For example, tell your minister that his birthday is considered to be a statutory holiday and therefore you do not expect him to come in to the office or do any work on that day. Do not take the day out of his regularly allotted days off or holiday time. This will only 'cost' you one day's worth of work - most of which your minister will likely make up for in the days preceding and following. I guarantee he will feel blessed, appreciated and extremely grateful for your 'birthday gift'. Or go the extra mile and throw in a gift card for his favorite coffee shop, book store or a nice restaurant. I've received this kind of gift from some of my leaders over the years, often at Christmas, and it can be a great token of affirmation.

Support

It is critical your minister has adequate support systems in place. Ministry is a lonely and challenging business. Your minister needs people he can talk to and relate to. People who understand what it's like to be in ministry. People he can be real with without worrying about how it might impact his congregation or his job. It's up to him to find a place that works for him. It's up to you to encourage him to do so and let him know you believe that it is valuable and a perfectly legitimate use of his time. Here are some of the best places for him to find that.

- Many cities have an Evangelical Ministerial Association your minister can join. Ministerial groups can have many different formats and goals. Some of these are very worthwhile, others are moderately so.

- More important than a formal large group you should encourage your minister to develop a small network of ministers that he can regularly connect with. Were it not for my good friends in S.E.S.P.U. my time in ministry would have been a lot more lonely and a lot more bleak. We don't do anything terribly special, we simply meet every couple months, talk about how our lives and ministries are going and pray for one another. Every minister would greatly benefit from a group like this, made up of his peers, I find three to six people is the optimum size. Never underestimate the value of being with a group of people who 'get' what you are going through. It could be with other ministers in your denomination or if there are not enough of those in your vicinity encourage your minister to find it with ministers from other churches in town. Remember one of the greatest struggles for your minister is finding opportunities to take his minister's hat off and just be himself. Finding a support group like this is one of those opportunities because everyone else there just wants to do the same thing.

FOR MINISTERS ONLY:

The first rule of S.E.S.P.U. is: You don't talk about S.E.S.P.U. In other words: What's said at S.E.S.P.U. stays at S.E.S.P.U. – this is absolutely essential. However, equally important is rule number two: No whining or bragging. We all talk about our challenges and frustrations and I think I've seen almost everyone in the group break down into tears at some point – myself included - and it needs to be a safe place for that. However, things are never allowed to digress into a giant gripe session. That doesn't do anyone any good. On the other hand, we have all been to preacher retreats with guys who can't shut up about how awesome their worship services are or how many people they've baptized this year or how their small groups have totally taken off. It's great to share successes and talk about what is working well, but only if it is done with the utmost humility and complete lack of hype.

- Another thing I have found extremely valuable in my ministry career is being connected with another minister who is older, wiser and more experienced. At my first church in that small little town I became good friends with the Free Methodist pastor who lived just down the street. My second church where I served as youth minister I benefited tremendously from the insights and encouragement of our senior minister. Over the last several years I have been blessed to be connected with a couple different ministers: one slightly older than myself the other more than 20 years my senior. I can say with full confidence that there is unequivocally no way I would still be in ministry if it were not for the input and influence of these men in my life.

FOR MINISTERS ONLY:
You need these support systems and it's up to you to go out and find them (or make them). If you want to survive in ministry you need a small group of ministers you can connect with regularly. You also need to find other older, wiser, been through the war and come out on the other side ministers who are willing to walk with you as your mentor or coach. I simply cannot stress this point enough. It is a make it or break it item.

REASON #7 (PART 2)

Stressors

The next two items follow a similar theme. They're both based on the following principle: Your minister needs time off, time away, time to recharge his batteries. Ministry can be extremely draining, especially since a fairly high percentage of ministers are introverts in an extremely people oriented business. The reality of ministry is that the work is never done. There will always be more to do. There will always be more time to be spent. There will always be more needs to fill. And without regularly and deliberately stepping away, your minister will be ground to exhaustion. Even Jesus regularly went off to a lonely place by himself – that should tell us something.

Imagine yourself in a rowboat out in the middle of the lake. There is a hole in the bottom of the boat and water is gradually seeping in. Thankfully you have a bucket and so you begin to bail water out of the boat. You bail the water out continually at a consistent rate, making good progress but little by little you are falling behind. As time goes by the water level in the rowboat rises and rises. Your use of the bucket is slowing how fast your boat is sinking, but it is sinking nonetheless. Eventually one of two things will happen: some mysterious force will come along and lift your boat out of the water long enough to allow all the water to drain out of the boat or the boat will sink and you along with. Technically, option three is you row the boat to shore, get out, walk away and leave it all behind – but that's what we're trying to avoid here.

Sabbaths

Every now and then I will be sitting in a group going through one of those icebreaker activities and I will be prompted to answer the question, "What is your favorite day of the week?" My answer is startling to most people, particularly fans of Garfield, because my favorite day of the week is Monday. Equally shocking is the revelation that my least favorite day of the week is usually Friday. Let me explain how I end up here:

Tuesday to Thursday are just normal work days for me. They're not my favorite days, but not my worst either. You would assume Sundays would be at the top of the list for a minister and some weeks it is, or at least close to it. However many weeks it is a constant battle that takes conscious effort to keep my Sundays a heavenly day of worship rather than just a hectic day of work. Your minister's to do list is long on Sundays. So many people to talk to. So many issues to discuss. So many wrinkles to get ironed out. And then there is the stress of standing up in front of all of you and speaking for the appropriate amount of time, with proper tone and adequate enthusiasm, not to mention solid Biblical exegesis, profound real life application and attention grabbing – but not showy – presentation. Even after all these years I still get the cold hands before preaching and the sweats after from the stress of it all. Even after the "amen", the bulk of the rest of my Sunday, especially in the school year, is usually filled up with church related work of one kind or another as well.

That leaves Friday, Saturday and Monday. Saturday is usually my day off, though it often gets filled with some church related activities and even on the best of weeks most of my Saturday evening is spent in sermon polishing and memorization. My brain just can't keep what I studied on Friday afternoon fresh until Sunday morning.

Friday is the worst day of my week because I get to the office, look at my white board and say, "What absolutely has to be done by Sunday and what can wait until next week?" It is also the day I assess how much work I have left to do on Sunday's sermon and match up how many office hours remain. They never match. Ironically, it also seems to be the day when the highest number of unexpected things happen.

This week my Saturday is fully booked with other things – hanging out with church friends, my son's football game and a church BBQ in the evening. Therefore the weight of Friday is multiplied by knowing whatever I don't get done today, I won't get back to until nine or ten p.m. tomorrow. That doesn't account for all the unanticipated interruptions, urgent emails and unexpected visitors.

And that leaves Monday. Monday is my sabbath, my true day off.

SIDENOTE: You may have noticed my regular schedule doesn't allow me two full days off back to back. Most ministers I have talked to are in a similar situation. Not only can this lack of back-to-back days of rest away from the job wear your minister down physically over time, it can also impact him mentally. My weekend just doesn't feel the same way it feels to someone with a Monday to Friday job and therefore I usually don't greet it with the same enthusiasm some of you do. Those of you who have shift work jobs including regular weekend rotations know what I'm talking about. I confess there have been times when I've felt a little resentful of those who are celebrating the arrival of the weekend on Friday (oh you radio DJs, how you mock me!). Unless I've been very deliberate about things, it doesn't take much for bitterness to be transferred into my ministry and my church.

In the row boat analogy above, the boat is ministry and the bucket you are using to bail water out is a sabbath. As long as your minister keeps a sabbath routine he can slow the tide of the rising water. Without a sabbath routine, he is just hastening the inevitable. When you hear the word Sabbath you most likely think of the Jewish holy day (or the 80s metal band). Let me explain further what I mean about having a sabbath routine. I believe it is critical that your minister has a _true_ day off. By true day off I mean the phone gets unplugged, the emails go unanswered. He does not read a book to prep for the next class he has to teach. He does not think about the next sermon he has to preach. He does not squeeze in an appointment. He doesn't do anything related to work. This is a day of rest and refreshing. Your minister needs at least one day every week where he can hit the reset button. My personal preference is to take Monday as my sabbath simply because after Sunday I'm usually toast. Your minister will know which day will work best for him. It's up to you to allow him to take it and encourage him to do so.

SIDENOTE: If your minister is like me, statutory holidays are somewhat useless to him. Let me explain why. First off, most ministers have to work on Sunday which tends to interrupt your long weekend. Moreover, my regular days off are Monday and Saturday. Whenever there is a stat, my day off gets bumped to Tuesday. But now I have a problem. If I take Tuesday as my true day off that means the first time I set foot inside my office or do anything work related is Wednesday morning. There is no way I will complete everything I need to do by quitting time on Friday. That means I will likely put in some extra hours in the evenings and spend most, if

SIDENOTE (cont):   not all, of Saturday working as well - all of which defeats the purpose of taking an extra day off on Tuesday. I'm much better off to work Tuesday and have Saturday free to spend with my family on their day off from work/school.

However, if I do not take Tuesday off I may get most, if not all, of my work done by the end of Friday, but that means I have essentially lost the benefit of having the stat holiday. When I began with my current church I explained this conundrum to my elders and asked if they would allow me to bank five of my statutory holidays each year to be used later as an additional week of vacation time. They were gracious and understanding enough to agree. So, instead of having stat holidays I essentially don't get any benefit from, I get an extra full week away from work which is a great benefit and renewal to me.

Although there could be some exceptions, I believe most ministers need a true day off each and every week. Much like in the boat illustration, you might be able to skip one scoop of the bucket, but if you miss more than that you will certainly start to see the water level rise and the boat start to sink.

Sabbaticals

Continuing with the rowboat analogy from above, sabbaticals are the moment when the boat gets lifted up out of the water and allowed to completely drain.

The more water there is in the boat, the longer it needs to be lifted out of the lake to completely drain and recover. When talk of sabbaticals comes up, many people see it as simply a ploy to swindle out a little, or a lot, more vacation time. That is not what a sabbatical is really all about. A sabbatical is also not primarily time for professional development or continuing education. Vacations, professional development, continuing education and mission work are all excellent things and your minister needs time, funds and opportunity to be involved in all of these, but a sabbatical is something totally different.

In an article written for Focus on the Family, Dale Wolyniak states, "A ministry sabbatical is ideally quite different from a traditional academic sabbatical or a sabbatical practiced in business. It is about the spirit and soul being refreshed, renewed and redirected." The word sabbatical looks like the word sabbath only longer, and that's a pretty good definition. A sabbatical has much of the same purpose and many of the same parameters as a weekly sabbath, only it lasts longer. Sabbaticals can take many shapes and forms but the goal is always the same: to lift the boat out of the water for long enough to allow the water to drain out.

The last several years I've gotten into the habit of taking a short sabbatical every summer either at a rented cabin or more recently at my father's campsite. The first couple times all I could afford, both in time and money, were three days. This year

I'm taking a full five days. In fact that's where I am right now – using my week of banked stats. I know what you're thinking, I'm not supposed to be working. The truth is, I'm not. One of the most refreshing things I do on these sabbaticals, aside from seeing as few people as possible, is write. Usually it's something fictional, this time it's for you. If I were planning our next sermon series or developing new small group material – *that* would be work. This, believe it or not, is refreshing for me.

Last year I took an unofficial short sabbatical in Malibu. "Must be nice!" you say. But it is not as cushy as it sounds. Technically the trip was booked on and paid for with professional development funds, however in my mind it was more of a sabbatical. You see, I attended the Bible lectures at Pepperdine University.

This event is the polar opposite of my cabin isolation. The lectures had thousands of people, but I hardly knew any of them and more importantly hardly any of them knew me or my church. So I didn't have to worry about being looked at as Mike the minister. I could just be an anonymous person in the crowd. I also stayed off campus by myself in a cheap little dive of a hotel and ate several times at Red Robin – both of which were incredibly nourishing for my soul.

For the record I did attend the classes and lectures. However, in the keynote sessions I generally sat as high up in the nosebleed section as I possibly could.

I looked for the grouping of chairs which would give me the maximum allowable space between me and any other person – it was not hard to find at that altitude. For the vast majority of the worship times I didn't sing, or even stand. Shhh, don't tell anyone. Why not you ask? Because it had been an especially stressful year and I was completely fried. In other words, my boat was all full, water was pouring over the gunnels and I was tired of bailing. So I just sat there and listened to the music. I just sat there and absorbed the worship. I did not have to worry about the problems with the sound equipment. I did not have to worry about the server who forgot to stand up when it was time to pass communion. I did not have to worry about remembering the lines for the sermon I was about to give or the critic I knew I was about to gift wrap some new ammunition for. I didn't have to do any of those things. I didn't have to be 'on'.

FOR MINISTERS ONLY:
What recreates you depends on who you are. I can't tell you what you will find refreshing. Neither can your church leaders. You have to figure out for yourself what places, people and activities fill up your tank and empty out your boat. Then you need to go there and do that as often as you have the chance.

In my experience and opinion, most ministers would benefit greatly from having a 3-5 day sabbatical at least twice a year. However, unless the church provides time, funds and encouragement, it is quite likely for most ministers this will never happen. Most ministers don't want to sacrifice what vacation time they have, because they need to spend that time with their family. In addition, the cost of a place to stay, travel and meals can add up frighteningly fast. If it comes down to a choice between using the money to take the kids to a motel with a water slide or allowing dad to go off into the woods by himself for a week, you can guess which one most ministers are going to choose.

SIDENOTE It is true your minister doesn't have to go away on his short sabbatical, but in my experience often times the best - sometimes only - way to really get refreshed is to physically get away, otherwise it is too easy for his short sabbatical to get filled up with a lot of other things that aren't necessarily providing the renewal he needs from this brief moment out of the water. And getting away, no matter where you go, always costs money.

Obviously, the challenge with sabbaticals is it takes time for the water to drain out the boat. The more water, the longer it takes. Every other summer we drive to my in-laws house in Iowa for the state fair. The journey is about 1200 miles from where we currently live and therefore we usually take two weeks of vacation to make the trek. I have discovered over the years it usually takes most of the first week for me to really step away from work and enjoy vacationing. The same holds true for sabbaticals.

Lifting the boat out of the water for a short spell is certainly worth it, but there's only so much decompression that can happen in three or four days. Sabbaths and short sabbaticals can buy your minister some time but at some point a longer break may be needed. If it is not available there may eventually come a time when your minister says, "You can live and function without me for three months now, or in the not so distant future you can live and function without any minister for three or six or twelve months as the search committee tries to find my replacement." It would be so much better for everyone if you were planning ahead instead of waiting for the moment to actually arrive.

```
SIDENOTE  Odds are pretty high most ministers won't
actually say this to you in so many words.   More
than likely they'll just keep doing their best to
bail out the boat until they eventually bail out
themselves.
```

In the article mentioned earlier, Wolyniak goes on to explain, "Many churches think of a sabbatical as merely a long vacation. However a sabbatical differs significantly from a vacation in many aspects...It should be a time to truly and completely disconnect from routines, responsibilities and relationships." Those who research and study these things suggest churches interested in the long term health and effectiveness of their minister should plan for a sabbatical of three or more months to be available to their minister every five to seven years. That seems to be the norm outside church circles as well.

I recently talked with a friend who works in a non-ministry field and is allotted a one year sabbatical after seven years of work. She is very excited to be finishing up year six. I realize there are a lot of jobs that don't offer sabbaticals of any kind, ever. However, given the nature of the work your minister is expected to do long term sabbaticals are absolutely invaluable. Earlier in this book, I shared the following statistic: most North American evangelical churches change ministers every four to seven years. It is no coincidence that those numbers coincide with the recommended timing of multi-month sabbaticals.

WHAT MIGHT HELP?

I know most churches don't have an unending supply of money and therefore it can be quite difficult rallying support for some of the expenses listed in these two chapters. However try not to base your decisions on what you can currently afford. In faith, base your decisions on what you think is right and proper. Base your decisions on what you think is best for your minister and your church. Base your decisions on what you believe God would want you to do. Then, if your bank account isn't sufficient enough to cover all the expenses your decision requires, make a strategy for how your church can get to that point. Here are some suggestions to make that happen:

- ***Talk to your minister.*** Figure out which of these needs is most urgent for him and his family and work on that item first.

- ***Do what you can.*** Maybe you can't send your minister to Maui for his sabbatical right now. That's okay just send him where you can. Maybe you can only afford to match RRSPs up to two percent of his base salary right now. That's okay, start with two percent now and work your way up to five percent in the next couple years. Do what you can now and intentionally build your way toward something greater in the future. Most ministers will understand and be willing to patiently wait if they know what is coming.

- ***Plan ahead.*** Perhaps your minister has only been with you 18 months and doesn't need a long term sabbatical yet. That's fine, go ahead and start putting money away so in four years when he's ready to throw in the towel you already have the means saved up to allow him an opportunity for refreshment and renewal. Our church sponsors a missionary family in South America. This family is scheduled to come home for a two month furlough every two years, but we don't wait until it's time for them to buy their tickets to try and come up with the money. Every month, since the day they left, we have been putting funds aside so when it's time for their furlough we are prepared.

For any important item your congregation can't afford at the moment make a detailed plan of how you're going to get there and then do everything you can to stick to the plan.

FOR MINISTERS ONLY:
It is your job to watch the fuel gauge on your gas tank and take action before the needle dips too low. Pay attention to your moods and energy levels. Is there a particular day of the week that you feel consistently low? I realized about a decade ago, thanks to the observations of a good friend, I almost always bottom out in early October. I don't know why, it just seems to happen that way. Be aware of yourself and adjust your schedule and activities accordingly.

THE END IS NEAR

The chapter heading above applies to this book but it *does not have to* apply to your minister. Your church is not perfect – your minister is well aware of this fact. Your minister is not perfect either – pretty much everyone is aware of this fact, including your minister. No one should expect either of them to be perfect. Every job has its challenges. Every work environment has room for improvement. You, no doubt, have a list of things you'd like to change about your own working conditions or job description. This book does not presume to give you all the answers or claim to know the 'right' way to handle everything. My singular desire is to give you a sense of what it is like to be in full time church ministry and to provide a vehicle for you, as a church leader, and your minister(s) to begin a dialogue about the most effective ways to expand his longevity and effectiveness in your congregation.

The good news is even if your minister is considering quitting, odds are fairly good he doesn't *want* to. After all, there are many rewarding and satisfying blessings a minister gets from being in ministry. Your minister wouldn't be in ministry in the first place if he didn't have a heart for it. Besides, all of his experience, expertise and education are in ministry. If he moves to a different career he will be starting from scratch all over again, bottom rung of the ladder, competing for jobs against 25 year olds fresh out of university with degrees relevant to their field. In the end, most ministers who leave ministry and move into other professions do it not because they want to, but more because they can't see any alternative. They say things like:

- I just can't handle being criticized for everything I do
- I just can't stand having all my work hijacked by people with their own agendas
- I just can't stand spending all my time and energy just keeping the wheels turning and the lights on
- I just can't work in an environment where my leaders don't trust me and I don't trust them
- I just can't provide for my family on what they pay me
- I just can't keep going and going, giving and giving. My well is dry. My tank is empty.

If they could see their way out of all this without leaving ministry that would likely be their preference. If they could see legitimate hope things would change and improve they'd probably stay. This is your quest: to give your minister hope, but not a false hope. To give your minister a promise, but not an empty promise. Your challenge is to convince your minister you want him to stay and you will do everything in your power to make that possible for him. Here are some initial steps to communicating that message.

- **Say it.** Tell your minister in no uncertain terms, "We do not want you to leave or feel like you have to quit and do something else. We appreciate the work you are doing for the Kingdom and if you ever need anything just let us know." Just this past Sunday I was talking to one of our church leaders about my slack preaching schedule over the next four weeks. I explained it wasn't really on purpose, but it was just the way everything happened to line up. Without any prompting whatsoever she said, "That's okay. You need a break sometimes. We don't want you to burn out." Take it from me: regular, sincere, comments like that go a long way to talking your minister off the ledge.

- **Put your money where your mouth is.** As encouraging as your comments can be to your minister – and they can be incredibly encouraging – at some point along the way your church is going to eventually need to make like Cuba Gooding Jr. in Jerry McGuire and "Show me the money." As an old missionary friend of my father once said – when the support check he and his wife were depending on to live didn't come, again – "I know you're supposed to be able live on hugs and kisses, but the ol' girl ain't what she used to be." Your minister will value your verbal expressions of appreciation, but at the same time he still has to pay his bills. If he doesn't have opportunities for professional development his well will run dry. If he doesn't have regular sabbath and sabbatical opportunities his boat will sink.

- **Do it. Just do it. Do it.** This may be the most difficult step of all. Encouraging words are great! Better financial packages are wonderful! But the single most important thing you can do to preserve your minister is step up. Develop volunteers, divert hijackers, dissuade critics, shelter him from the fishbowl, free him from non-essential plates and build a relationship of trust with him. I have seen on several occasions, ministers who were in churches where people often stated they were happy he was there, churches that were quite generous in regard to both his salary, benefits and working budget and yet the minister still packed it all in. I have asked some of them why and they say, "The people just wouldn't step up or show up. They wouldn't personally invest. They would never actually *do* anything." If you want to know how to make the absolute biggest impact upon your minister – and the rest of your church and your community for that matter – then show up, dive in, help out, step up, chip in, invest, participate, do.

I hope, with all my heart, this book has been helpful and inspiring to you. I hope that you walk away excited about the potential in your congregation when it is being led by a healthy, cared for, defended, refreshed and loved minister. I hope you don't put this book down and think ministers are all a bunch of spoiled whiners who want the whole world handed to them on a silver platter while they sit back on a beach in Cancun being *(sarcasm alert)* 'spiritually refreshed'.

If you do, take it out on me not your own minister – he had nothing to do with it and I'm sure the last thing he needs is for you to rake him over the coals because of something you read in some book that some doorknob he doesn't even know wrote. There's plenty of room in my Critics File for your *'encouraging'* letter. Just ignore how my Critics File looks suspiciously similar to a paper shredder. If you found some value in what you read – which I sincerely hope you did – then please, take it, apply it, share it and use it. Our ministers are a precious resource which is fast becoming a rare commodity. Let us do *our best* to make sure they can be at *their best,* so the church can accomplish *His best.*

THE CONVERSATION

CONTINUES...

Check out the Holy Toast **WEBSITE** (**holytoastbook.wordpress.com**) for additional content, resources and an opportunity to give your feedback and comments on the book.

Follow the author on **TWITTER**: **@HolyToastBook** or tweet your comments, thoughts and favorite quote to using **#HolyToast**

Like us (**Holy Toast Book**) on **FACEBOOK** and share our page with others in your social network

SPECIAL THANKS TO:

My Wife & Kids
My Family & In-laws
S.E.S.P.U.
Kirk Ruch
Steve McMillan
Scott Roberts
Blair Roberts
Frank Wheeler
Jennifer Jacoby-Smith
Swift Current Church of Christ
Dauphin Church of Christ
Wawota Church of Christ
South Burnaby Church of Christ
Saskatoon Church of Christ
Western Christian College
York College
And many others...

Proof

Made in the USA
Charleston, SC
23 April 2015